Expert Tips to Unleash the Full Potential of SAP® Controlling

Ashish Sampat

Thank you for purchasing this book from Espresso Tutorials!

Like a cup of espresso coffee, Espresso Tutorials SAP books are concise and effective. We know that your time is valuable and we deliver information in a succinct and straightforward manner. It only takes our readers a short amount of time to consume SAP concepts. Our books are well recognized in the industry for leveraging tutorial-style instruction and videos to show you step by step how to successfully work with SAP.

Check out our YouTube channel to watch our videos at
https://www.youtube.com/user/EspressoTutorials.

If you are interested in SAP Finance and Controlling, join us at
http://www.fico-forum.com/forum2/
to get your SAP questions answered and contribute to discussions.

Related titles from Espresso Tutorials:

- ▶ Martin Munzel: New SAP® Controlling Planning Interface
  http://5011.espresso-tutorials.com
- ▶ Michael Esser: Investment Project Controlling with SAP®
  http://5008.espresso-tutorials.com
- ▶ Stefan Eifler: Quick Guide to SAP® CO-PA (Profitability Analysis)
  http://5018.espresso-tutorials.com
- ▶ Kermit Bravo & Scott Cairncross: SAP® Enterprise Performance Management (EPM) Add-In
  http://5042.espresso-tutorials.com
- ▶ Paul Ovigele: Reconciling SAP® CO-PA to the General Ledger
  http://5040.espresso-tutorials.com
- ▶ Tanya Duncan: Practical Guide to SAP® CO-PC (Product Cost Controlling)
  http://5064.espresso-tutorials.com
- ▶ Ashish Sampat: First Steps in SAP® Controlling (CO)
  http://5069.espresso-tutorials.com
- ▶ Rosana Fonseca: Practical Guide to SAP® Material Ledger (ML)
  http://5116.espresso-tutorials.com
- ▶ Tanya Duncan: The Essential SAP® Career Guide—Hitting the Ground Running
  http://5142.espresso-tutorials.com

Ashish Sampat
Expert Tips to Unleash the Full Potential of SAP Controlling

ISBN:	9-781-5369-9097-3
Editor:	Christine Parizo
Cover Design:	Philip Esch, Martin Munzel
Cover Photo:	fotolia: #94818260 (c) Trifonenko Ivan
Interior Design:	Johann-Christian Hanke

All rights reserved.

1st Edition 2016, Gleichen

© 2016 by Espresso Tutorials GmbH

URL: *www.espresso-tutorials.com*

Feedback
We greatly appreciate any kind of feedback you have concerning this book. Please mail us at *info@espresso-tutorials.com*.

Table of Contents

Preface

During launch of my first book, "First Steps in SAP Controlling (CO)," the Espresso Tutorials team asked me if I would be interested in writing another book—this time, a book that will include tips in SAP Controlling for advanced practitioners. I thought through the proposal and accepted the offer. After all, a book for experts was the next logical step to a beginners' book.

This book is meant to give a few tools and tips to practitioners that will help them unleash the full potential of SAP Controlling. It is also intended to boost the productivity of their SAP installations.

I love working at different client sites and studying their SAP designs— each design is unique. Starting with the organizational structure and then moving to master data and transaction data, it is nice to visualize the big picture and see how it all fits together. I have tried to incorporate many of these lessons and best practices in both my books.

SAP teams continuously face the challenge of keeping pace with the constant innovation and improvement in SAP's product features. The goal of "keeping the lights on," as well as continuous improvement, becomes even more challenging when there are competing business requirements.

Many things are likely to change with the advent of groundbreaking innovations like S/4 HANA. However, my belief is that a good understanding of the fundamental concepts of SAP's core product will go a long way in making the most out of the system.

I would like to thank the Espresso Tutorials team for giving me an opportunity to write another book for them. I also want to thank my family, friends, colleagues, and fellow SAP consultants for providing encouragement and support while I wrote this book.

I dedicate this book to my parents, from whom I learned to never forget one's roots and humble beginnings.

Introduction

Like this book's predecessor, *First Steps in SAP Controlling (CO)*, this book will also be told in case study approach.

Global Confectioners, Inc. (GCI) is a fictional organization that manufactures chocolates and other confectionery products. GCI has recently acquired another company, National Confectioners, Limited (NCL). These two companies are in the process of integrating their operations. We will use the GCI and NCL integration as a case study to walk through real-life scenarios using SAP Controlling at a manufacturing facility.

Alex, the plant cost analyst at GCI who was introduced in the first book, continues his journey of learning SAP Controlling. Having spent a few months in his new role at GCI, Alex now has a good grasp on the subject matter. The reader will come across the following characters at GCI and NCL in this book:

- ▶ Alex—Plant Cost Analyst at GCI
- ▶ Bob—Plant Controller and Alex's manager at CGI
- ▶ Carl—Manufacturing Manager at CGI
- ▶ Dave—Inventory Controller at CGI
- ▶ Erin—Finance IT support at CGI
- ▶ Frank—Plant Controller at NCL
- ▶ Greg—Manufacturing Manager at NCL

Alex and his team will interact with each other while learning expert tricks and tips on various topics like configuration, master data, transaction processing, period-end closing, and reporting.

Each tip will be explained using the following criteria:

- ▶ What it does (functionality overview)
- ▶ Where it will help you (benefits)
- ▶ Why you should use it (what pain points will be addressed)
- ▶ How to use it (configuration/data/cutover steps to implement this tip)

This book is ideal for SAP Controlling professionals who want to learn expert tips to optimize their system performance, whether in the configuration area or the reconciliation and reporting areas. After learning basics of SAP Controlling, this is the next logical step in the journey. Screenshots from a test system are provided so that the reader is able to visualize the functionality and implementation steps effectively.

We have added a few icons to highlight important information. These include:

Tip

Tips highlight information concerning more details about the subject being described and/or additional background information.

Example

Examples help illustrate a topic better by relating it to real world scenarios.

Attention

Attention notices draw attention to information that you should be aware of when you go through the examples from this book on your own.

Finally, a note concerning the copyright: all screenshots printed in this book are the copyright of SAP SE. All rights are reserved by SAP SE. Copyright pertains to all SAP images in this publication. For simplification, we will not mention this specifically underneath every screenshot.

1 Optimize period-end closing

This chapter covers tips to optimize period-end closing, often referred to as month-end close or financial close.

Period-end closing is an important task in an organization's operations. Period-end close allows the finance team to perform various coordinated tasks that allow it to determine the financial health of the organization. It provides the management with a report of what occurred in the most recent fiscal period.

Having performed month-end close over many years, most organizations may have streamlined it into a successful routine. Yet there may be organizations that struggle to coordinate month-end close tasks effectively. Closing books too quickly without quality checks may result in inaccuracies, whereas too slow month-end closing may not allow enough time for course correction. Optimizing period-end close is therefore necessary to give management an accurate financial picture of the state of operations

1.1 Synchronize FI, CO, and MM periods

Global Confectioners, Inc. (GCI) and National Confectioners, Limited (NCL) are in the process of merging their operations, including their information systems and accounting. The GCI and NCL teams are discussing how to design their processes for period-end closing. GCI and NCL will have separate company codes, and they will continue to operate independently from operations and finance standpoints.

"Can you help me understand what FI, CO, and MM periods in SAP are? And how can we use them effectively in our close process?" Frank asked Alex. Frank is the Controller of NCL, which was acquired by GCI. Alex has now spent more than a year as the Plant Cost Analyst at GCI. Alex is usually the go-to person for Frank for any questions related to SAP Controlling.

"Sure, let's go through this document together. It will help explain the process," replied Alex.

1.1.1   What FI, CO, and MM period locks do

MMPV—Materials Management (MM) period:

Transaction MMPV—*MM Period Roll* job—runs on midnight of the first day of the accounting period (e.g., 10/01/2015 at 00:01:00 hours). What MMPV essentially does is open up the new MM period, thereby allowing materials-related entries in the new accounting period (e.g., period 10 will be opened).

Figure 1.1 shows transaction MMPV in two separate screens. MMPV was run first for company code range GCI1 to GCI2, followed by company code NCL1.

The menu path is as follows: LOGISTICS • MATERIALS MANAGEMENT • MATERIAL MASTER • OTHER • MMPV—CLOSE PERIOD.

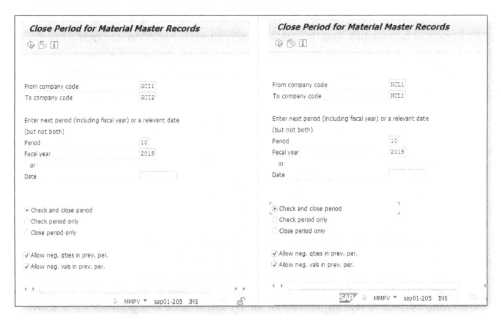

Figure 1.1: MMPV—Close MM period GCI1, GCI2, and NCL1

Two MM periods are open at any time. When transaction MMPV runs and opens the new period, it closes the period immediately preceding (e.g., when period 10 is opened, eight is automatically closed, thereby leaving MM periods 9 and 10 open). At this stage, no materials-related entries can be made to MM period 8, whether FI and CO period locks for period 8 are open or not.

Figure 1.2 shows transaction SE16 for table MARV. Periods 10/2015 and 9/2015 are open from a materials management standpoint. The system recognizes 12/2014 as the last period of the previous fiscal year. No postings can be carried to 12/2014, though. (Note: access to transaction SE16 may be restricted to select IT personnel.)

Cl.	CoCd	Year	Pe	FYr	MP	FYr	LM	ABp	DBp	Changed by	Last Chg	Time
850	GCI1	2015	10	2015	9	2014	12	X		SAMPAT	10/22/2015	03:42:16
850	GCI2	2015	10	2015	9	2014	12	X		SAMPAT	10/22/2015	03:43:37
850	NCL1	2015	10	2015	9	2014	12	X		SAMPAT	10/22/2015	03:51:45

Data Browser: Table MARV: *3 of*   *3 Hits*

Check Table...   SE16   sap01-205   INS

Figure 1.2: SE16—Table MARV—MM periods for GCI1, GCI2, NCL1

All goods movement transactions for the new period will stop if the MM period for the new month is not opened at the correct time. Therefore, transaction MMPV is scheduled as a batch job via its underlying program RMMMPERI. Usually, a select few IT employees have access to MMPV in the production system as a backup. Once an MM period is closed for an older month, it is usually not advisable to re-open it, as doing so may lead to inconsistencies in the system.

It is also very important to keep FI and CO period locks for the new period open; otherwise, MM postings for the new period will fail.

OB52—Financial Accounting (FI) period lock:

FI period lock can be maintained for various *Account types* (like K-Vendor, D-Customer, A-Assets, S-GL Accounts, M-Materials, etc.). Most account types for new FI periods are opened a couple of days prior to the MM period (e.g., FI period lock for period 10 should be opened on 9/29 or 9/30). The existing FI period is kept open until period-end close tasks are completed over a few days in the new month. Vendor Accounts for current period are usually locked early, and Invoice Verification posting can be done only when MM periods are opened for period 10. Materials and GL Accounts are open for a few more days. Two periods are open to facilitate closure during this time. During these few days, postings can be made to the previous period, provided the relevant Account Types are open. Once FI period is closed, no postings can be made in the previous period.

FI period is controlled for each posting period variant. *Posting period variant* is used to control which accounting period is to be open for posting. In other words, a posting period that is closed cannot take any further postings, thereby ensuring that prior periods are untouched. Posting period variant is attached at the company code level.

Technically, FI periods can be re-opened and closed any number of times if there is a genuine business need. This is usually not encouraged for obvious reasons like the risk of changing financial results already reported, reconciliation purposes, etc. *Authorization group* can be used to restrict postings to general posting in FI versus special posting in FI. Certain users (generally members of the finance department that are involved with the close process) with special access can post to prior FI periods.

Figure 1.3 provides an example of an FI period lock. The scenario shown typically is applicable at the beginning of period 10, when period 9 closing is underway. As explained below, there are three period intervals. The first interval applies to a special set of users who have authorization to post to a prior period. The second interval is for general users; this interval is closed before the special users' interval is closed. The third interval is optional. If maintained, the third interval is applicable for CO to FI postings, e.g., distribution/assessment postings that occur in CO and are sent over to FI. If interval 3 is left blank, then intervals 1 and 2 are considered for CO to FI postings.

FI period lock can be maintained using transaction OB52. Alternate transactions S_ALR_87003642 and FAGL_EHP4_T001B_COFI may also be used, depending on security access setup. Note: depending on the system version, transaction OB52/S_ALR_87003642 may or may not have the third interval visible. Transaction FAGL_EHP4_T001B_COFI will always show the third interval.

Figure 1.3: OB52—FI period lock example

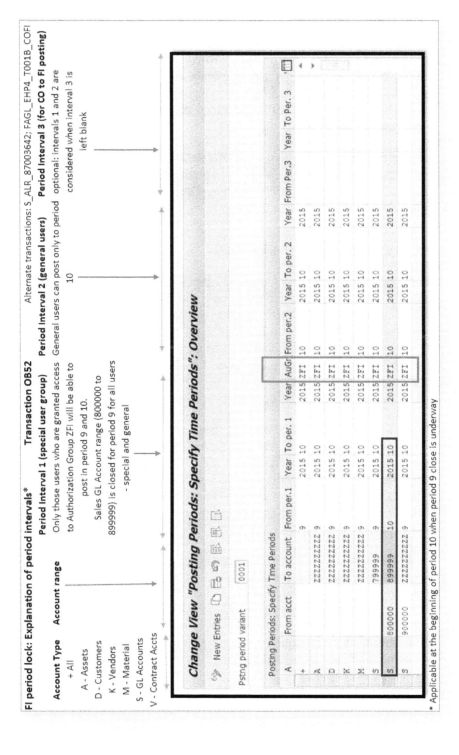

The menu path is as follows: ACCOUNTING • FINANCIAL ACCOUNTING • GEN-ERAL LEDGER • REPORTING • TAX REPORTS • FRANCE • SALES/PURCHASES TAX RETURNS • SALES/PURCHASES TAX RETURNS • OB52—CLOSE POSTING PERIODS IN GENERAL LEDGER. Note: upon review of the menu path, it may seem like this transaction is applicable only for France, but this is not the case. OB52 is applicable for all countries and regions (e.g., at the SAP system/client level).

The menu path for FAGL_EHP4_T001B_COFI is as follows: ACCOUNTING • FINANCIAL ACCOUNTING • GENERAL LEDGER • ENVIRONMENT • CURRENT SETTINGS • FAGL_EHP4_T001B_COFI—OPEN AND CLOSE POSTING PERIODS

OKP1—Controlling (CO) period lock:

CO period lock can be maintained by various CO Transactions (not to be confused with an SAP transaction code, CO Transaction here refers to controlling *business transaction*). One Transaction that affects postings from FI to CO is "CO-through postings in FI" (COIN). If COIN is locked in CO, then no postings can occur in FI or CO, even when the FI period is open. It is therefore important to open the CO period lock immediately upon opening the FI Period lock for the next period (e.g., the CO period lock for period 10 should be opened on 9/29 or 9/30).

CO period lock is applicable only for those accounts that are created as cost elements, generally on the P&L side. This would mean that balance sheet postings ignore the CO period lock. This would mean that the FI Period lock has a broader impact than the CO period lock. Even after the FI period is locked, there are certain transactions that can be carried out within Controlling (like Assessments and Activity Allocations), which are specific to CO.

FI and CO periods are generally maintained by a single team in the Finance department. MM periods are controlled by the batch job mentioned above.

Figure 1.4 shows the CO Period lock screen from transaction OKP1. Certain business transactions are open for period 9 while financial close for that period is in progress. All business transactions are open for period 10 (the current period)

The menu path is as follows: ACCOUNTING • CONTROLLING • COST CENTER ACCOUNTING • ENVIRONMENT • PERIOD LOCK • OKP1—CHANGE

Change Actual Period Lock : Edit

Lock Period   Lock Transaction   Unlock Period   Unlock Transaction

Controlling Area   GCI1 Global Confectioners, Inc
Fiscal Year   2015

Period locks

Transaction	01	02	03	04	05	06	07	08	09	10	11	12	13	14	15	16
ABC Actual process assessment	✓	✓	✓	✓	✓	✓	✓	✓	✓	☐	✓	✓	✓	✓	✓	✓
Actual Overhead Assessment	✓	✓	✓	✓	✓	✓	✓	✓	☐	☐	✓	✓	✓	✓	✓	✓
Actual Overhead Distribution	✓	✓	✓	✓	✓	✓	✓	✓	☐	☐	✓	✓	✓	✓	✓	✓
Actual Periodic Repostings	✓	✓	✓	✓	✓	✓	✓	✓	✓	☐	✓	✓	✓	✓	✓	✓
Actual activity allocation	✓	✓	✓	✓	✓	✓	✓	✓	✓	☐	✓	✓	✓	✓	✓	✓
Actual cost center accrual	✓	✓	✓	✓	✓	✓	✓	✓	✓	☐	✓	✓	✓	✓	✓	✓
Actual cost center split	✓	✓	✓	✓	✓	✓	✓	✓	✓	☐	✓	✓	✓	✓	✓	✓
Actual cost distrib. cost obj.	✓	✓	✓	✓	✓	✓	✓	✓	✓	☐	✓	✓	✓	✓	✓	✓
Actual inverse activity alloc.	✓	✓	✓	✓	✓	✓	✓	✓	✓	☐	✓	✓	✓	✓	✓	✓
Actual non-alloc. activities	✓	✓	✓	✓	✓	✓	✓	✓	✓	☐	✓	✓	✓	✓	✓	✓
Actual overhead (periodic)	✓	✓	✓	✓	✓	✓	✓	✓	✓	☐	✓	✓	✓	✓	✓	✓
Actual price calculation	✓	✓	✓	✓	✓	✓	✓	✓	☐	☐	✓	✓	✓	✓	✓	✓
Actual settlement	✓	✓	✓	✓	✓	✓	✓	✓	☐	☐	✓	✓	✓	✓	✓	✓
Actual template allocation	✓	✓	✓	✓	✓	✓	✓	✓	☐	☐	✓	✓	✓	✓	✓	✓
Assessment to CO-PA	✓	✓	✓	✓	✓	✓	✓	✓	☐	☐	✓	✓	✓	✓	✓	✓
Automat. WIP/results analysis	✓	✓	✓	✓	✓	✓	✓	✓	☐	☐	✓	✓	✓	✓	✓	✓
CO Through-postings from FI	✓	✓	✓	✓	✓	✓	✓	✓	☐	☐	✓	✓	✓	✓	✓	✓
COPA: TOP-DOWN: Actuals	✓	✓	✓	✓	✓	✓	✓	✓	✓	☐	✓	✓	✓	✓	✓	✓
Down payment	✓	✓	✓	✓	✓	✓	✓	✓	✓	☐	✓	✓	✓	✓	✓	✓
Enter statistical key figures	✓	✓	✓	✓	✓	✓	✓	✓	✓	☐	✓	✓	✓	✓	✓	✓
Interest calculation (actual)	✓	✓	✓	✓	✓	✓	✓	✓	✓	☐	✓	✓	✓	✓	✓	✓
JV Actual assessment	✓	✓	✓	✓	✓	✓	✓	✓	✓	☐	✓	✓	✓	✓	✓	✓

SAP ▷ OKP1 ▼ sap01-205 INS

Figure 1.4: OKP1—CO period lock example

1.1.2 Where period locks will help you in SAP

All the three period locks must work in harmony; otherwise, there will be inconsistencies, including goods movement errors in the system.

MM period is controlled at the company code level, FI period at the posting period level (the company code is attached to the posting period level), and CO period at the controlling area level.

Alex, Erin, and Frank reviewed the design decision document that was prepared for the integration of GCI and NCL:

▶ **Company code**—NCL will be set up as a separate company code. Management would like to maintain NCL as an independent entity while leveraging the reach of GCI's distribution network.

▶ **Chart of accounts**—GCI will continue to use the existing chart of accounts. This will facilitate consolidation of reporting of all company codes.

▶ **Operating concern, fiscal year variant, and controlling area** — NCL will use GCI's operating concern, fiscal year variant, and controlling area, given that the management wants a single internal reporting view of the combined operations of GCI and NCL.

Even though GCI and NCL will have separate company codes, they plan to follow the same close calendar. Therefore, it makes sense to assign the NCL company code to the same posting period variant as that of GCI and allow for common maintenance of the FI period lock. Additionally, since both these company codes share a common controlling area (implying single maintenance of the CO period lock in OKP1), there is even more synergy in using a single posting period variant. Lastly, with regard to the MM period, it is maintained at the company code level and hence, both GCI and NCL will each need to run MMPV via its underlying program RMMMPERI.

1.1.3 Why you use period locks in SAP

Ensuring accurate cut-off of various processes for month-end, including Sales, AR, AP, Fixed Assets, and Inventory movement transactions, is important for a smooth financial month-end close. Communicating such cut-off dates to various stakeholders across processes and functions is important. This will help schedule month-end close tasks around these cut-off dates, leveraging features of FI, CO, and MM period locks.

1.1.4 How to use period locks in SAP

Mapping financial month-end close processes needs to be covered right from the business blueprint phase of the SAP implementation project.

Cross-functional business and IT teams should review current month-end close processes and carefully map them to the future processes.

If you are trying to optimize or fine-tune your current month-end task list, you can leverage the functionality of FI, CO, and MM period locks.

1.2 Automate WIP, Variance, Settlement

There could be several orders that are open at month-end, and several could be completed. Open orders need to be carried forward using Work-in-Process (WIP), whereas variances on completed orders need to be settled.

A Production/Process Order is assigned various statuses in its lifecycle. For example, order status CRTD (created) is set at the time of order creation, REL (released) is set at the time of release, PDLV (partially delivered) is set at the time of partial delivery, DLV (delivered) is set at the time of final delivery, and TECO (technically complete) is set at the time of technical completion. Order status determines what type of business transactions can be allowed, and it therefore plays an important role in the order lifecycle.

"What other manufacturing and related costing tasks do I need to be aware of during month-end close?" Frank asked Alex during their weekly meeting.

"Process order is our cost object where we collect all our costs," Alex responded. "We must calculate Work-in-Process, Variance, and Settlement on all our orders."

1.2.1 What WIP, Variance, and Settlement do

Work-in-Process (WIP) calculation on orders:

Incomplete (or *Work-in-process*—WIP) orders: Orders which have costs posted against them, and the system status is neither DLV (delivered) nor TECO (technically complete), are considered incomplete. Such orders will qualify for WIP calculation. WIP is calculated using the following transactions:

- ► KKAO—WIP mass processing
- ► KKAQ—WIP mass display
- ► KKAX—WIP individual processing
- ► KKAY—WIP individual display

The menu path is as follows: CONTROLLING • PRODUCT COST CONTROL-LING • COST OBJECT CONTROLLING • PRODUCT COST BY ORDER • PERIOD-END CLOSING • SINGLE FUNCTIONS • WORK IN PROCESS • COLLECTIVE PRO-CESSING • KKAO—CALCULATE.

Variance calculation on orders

Completed orders: Orders with a system status of either DLV (delivered), TECO (technically completed), or both are considered to be complete. Such orders will qualify for *variance calculation*. As the name suggests, the system calculates target versus actual variances. Targets are deter-mined based on the standard cost estimate. Variance is calculated using the following transactions:

- ► KKS1—Variance mass processing
- ► KKS2—Variance individual processing

The menu path is as follows: CONTROLLING • PRODUCT COST CONTROL-LING • COST OBJECT CONTROLLING • PRODUCT COST BY ORDER • PERIOD-END CLOSING • SINGLE FUNCTIONS • VARIANCES • KKS1—COLLECTIVE PRO-CESSING.

WIP and Variance calculation do not post entries!

 WIP and Variance calculation transactions do not post any financial entries; they merely calculate the amount of WIP variance to be settled. Financial postings occur when the settlement transaction is executed.

Settlement of orders:

Once WIP and variance calculation is complete, the next step is to post these values to financial accounting using the *settlement* transaction. Costs are settled to a specific object that is maintained in the settlement rule.

Settlement rule is governed by the order type and the nature of activity/production performed on the order. Whereas most orders would settle to material, some orders may settle to a cost center, an internal order, a GL Account, or a work breakdown structure (WBS) element.

Settlement is performed using the following transactions:

▶ CO88—Settlement mass processing.

▶ KO88—Settlement individual processing.

The menu path is as follows: CONTROLLING • PRODUCT COST CONTROLLING • COST OBJECT CONTROLLING • PRODUCT COST BY ORDER • PERIOD-END CLOSING • SINGLE FUNCTIONS • SETTLEMENT • CO88—COLLECTIVE PROCESSING.

Financial postings at settlement

 Financial posting for WIP: Settlement posts WIP entries to the P&L and balance sheet accounts configured for carrying forward balances to the next month. Cost display in COR3 is not affected (that is, the WIP amount is not reflected as a separate line in the COR3 cost display). WIP values will automatically be reversed during the subsequent period's settlement once the orders are set to TECO/DLV status. (Orders may not always be completed in the subsequent month but may be completed after several months, depending on the industry and the nature of product and/or production process).

Financial posting for Variance: Settlement posts variance entries to production order variance accounts and factory output production (also known as production value) GL Accounts.

Note: An order usually has either WIP or variance posting in a particular month. An order may get both a WIP and a variance posting in the month in which an incomplete order is completed.

1.2.2 Where WIP, Variance, and Settlement help you

Frequency and mode of execution:

As noted earlier, WIP and Variance calculations do not post any financial entries; postings occur only at the time of settlement. This would imply that one could run WIP and Variance as many times as necessary. Settlement can also be run as many times as necessary, provided multiple postings for the same order are acceptable. Running these transactions daily may be overkill, so it may be run on a weekly or monthly basis.

Online execution (also referred to as foreground mode) of WIP, Variance, and Settlement transactions needs to be completed at the plant/controlling area level. Another way to handle frequent runs is to set up these transactions to run as batch jobs (also referred to as background mode).

1.2.3 Why run transactions in background mode

Scheduling background jobs will ensure these jobs are run automatically by the system. Background jobs create output (also known as spool) that can be reviewed by the business user.

Additionally, these transactions can be resource-intensive. Therefore, scheduling them during / off-peak hours helps maintain system performance during working hours when there could be a maximum load on the system.

1.2.4 Use batch jobs to run WIP, Variance, and Settlement

Background jobs can be set up using transaction SM36. This transaction may be controlled centrally by BASIS or the batch management team. Specific naming conventions need to be followed, depending on the company's internal processes.

The menu path is as follows: TOOLS • CCMS • BACKGROUND PROCESSING • SM36—DEFINE JOB

Program names for background runs are listed below. Variants need to be set up to ensure the jobs run for the desired selection criteria, like plant, year, period, and parallel processing.

- ► WIP: Program SAPKKA07BG
- ► Variance: Program RKKKS1N0
- ► Settlement: Program RKO7CO88

Background jobs can be reviewed by using transaction SM37. Figure 1.5 shows the status of WIP, Variance, and Settlement jobs executed in the background.

- ► ZCO101_SAPKKA07BG_WIP_WEEKLY
- ► ZCO102_RKKKS1N0_VAR_WEEKLY
- ► ZCO103_RKO7CO88_SETT_WEEKLY

Example naming convention ZXXNNN_PROG_PROC_VARIANT was followed. Where XX stands for team name (CO-Controlling); 101, 102, and 103 stand for job number sequence; PROG stands for program name, PROC stands for process name (e.g., WIP, Variance, Settlement); and variant name WEEKLY was used.

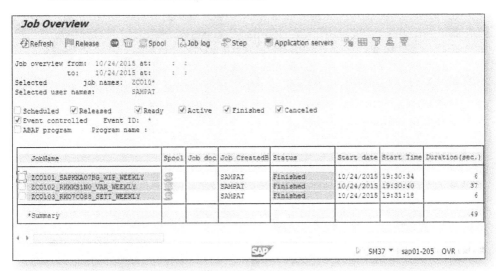

Figure 1.5: SM37—Job overview

In terms of timing and dependency, job 101 was set to run every Saturday at 19:30:00 hours, job 102 was made to be dependent on 101, and 103 was made dependent on 102. This would mean that 102 will start immediately once 101 finishes, and 103 will start immediately once 102 finishes.

23

The menu path is as follows: TOOLS • CCMS • BACKGROUND PROCESSING • SM37—JOBS—OVERVIEW AND ADMINISTRATION

Even when these jobs are scheduled to run in the background, it is a good idea to run them one final time before the books are closed. This can be done by using transactions KKAO, KKS1, and CO88 and running them in the background in quick succession. This will ensure any changes in transactional data after the batch job are accounted for and settled.

Order status change between jobs

It is possible that order(s) can change status between jobs due to additional transaction postings/user actions. To ensure accurate reconciliation and accounting, it is important that variance calculation and settlement be reversed for this order, followed by WIP, Variance, and Settlement.

As an example, Variance was calculated for an order that was in status DLV—delivered. After this, a goods receipt was reversed, thereby bringing the order in PDLV—partially delivered—status. In such a scenario, the suggested sequence of transactions for the given order would be KO88-reverse, KKS2-reverse, KKAX, KKS2, and KO88.

Orders for which status change can be identified use transactions COOISPI (Process order information system) and/or S_ALR_87013127 (Order selection).

1.3 Optimize cost allocation methods

A typical manufacturing facility incurs costs in various departments. For example, the maintenance department pays for the salary of its staff and spare parts to keep the machines running. Similarly, the information systems department pays for the salary of its staff and pays software licensing fees to keep the systems running. These are services rendered by support departments to the production department. Usually, the goal is to transfer costs from these service departments to production departments so that the costs are added to the price of the product. This transfer of costs internally within controlling is achieved using *allocations*.

There are two main types of allocations in controlling, distribution and assessments.

"And how about cost allocations? Do we need to do anything special from the month-end point of view?" Frank was curious.

"A lot of our plant costs are built into allocation cycles. This includes a lot of variable and fixed costs," Alex explained. "We are using a combination of assessment and distribution cycles."

1.3.1 What Distribution and Assessments do

Using *distribution*, the original, primary cost element is retained and passed on to the receivers. The sender and receiver information is documented with line items in the CO document.

Using *assessments*, the original cost elements are grouped together into assessment (secondary) cost elements and passed on to the receivers; original cost elements are not displayed on the receivers.

Figure 1.6 shows an example of a distribution cycle.

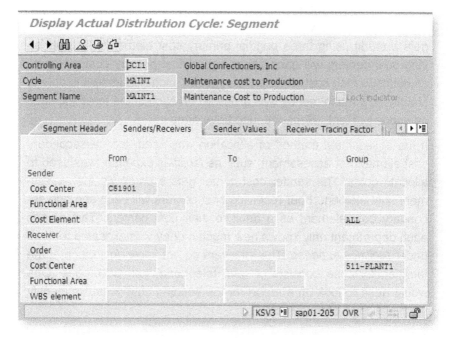

Figure 1.6: KSV3—Distribution MAINT sender and receiver

The sender and receiver rules are known as segments that are maintained in the cycles. Once an allocation cycle posts, the sender-receiver (segment) information is displayed in the controlling document.

The menu path is as follows: ACCOUNTING • CONTROLLING • COST CENTER ACCOUNTING • PERIOD-END CLOSING • SINGLE FUNCTIONS • ALLOCATIONS • DISTRIBUTION • EXTRAS • CYCLE • KSV3—DISPLAY.

Distribution versus assessment

Here is an example of a facilities department (one sending cost center) responsible for a building. This cost center incurs three primary costs: building rent, telephone expenses, and beverage expenses (such as tea and coffee) for staff working in that building. This building houses four departments: marketing, finance and accounting, purchasing, and human resources (four receiving cost centers). Costs should be allocated in predefined percentages for each department.

If the *distribution* method of allocation was used, then the same primary cost element was used to allocate costs. The sender cost center gets a credit using three original primary cost elements. Four receiving cost centers will each see three original primary cost elements as debits to their cost centers. This means each department is able to identify how much money was allocated on each of the three expense categories of rent, telephone, and beverages.

If the *assessment* method of allocation was used, then a secondary cost element for assessment, such as *facilities expense*, was used to allocate costs. The sender cost center gets a credit via the assessment cost element. Four receiving cost centers will each see one secondary cost element as a debit to their cost centers. This means each department only knows how much money was allocated to them under *facilities expense*. The receivers do not know how much of the facilities expense consists of rent, telephone, and beverages. One would need to look up a report for the sending cost center to identify the breakdown of these costs.

Whether an organization selects distribution, assessment, or both as its method of allocating cost center costs depends on the business requirement.

Performance concern:

Allocations cycles that have many sender/receiver relationships (also known as *segments*) can lead to long run times and result in performance issues.

SAP Note 1751885 (ALLOCATION-Description of database selection methods) provides guidance for which database selection method should be used and when. (Also referred as an OSS note, *OSS* is a short form of SAP's Online Support System, sometimes also referred to as Online Service System or Online Service Support, which provides easy access to SAP notes that may resolve some of the common problems faced by other customers. This may include bug fixes, answers to frequently asked questions, or even explanations for certain functions.) SAP note 1751885 explains how the various database selection methods work.

Excerpt from note: "When you select the correct database selection method, the runtimes may be significantly improved. Unfortunately, it is not possible to give general recommendations about which method is the fastest because the result depends on many factors (database, optimizer, number of objects, number of segments, type of definition of the cycle, and so on). As a rule, one method will not achieve the best result for all cycles."

1.3.2   Where optimizing run times will help you

Long run times can be a concern during month-end processing. There may be an increase in the overall month-end close timeline if a cycle has to be re-executed due to an error or a late transaction posting that necessitates re-processing cycles. Optimizing run times for allocation cycles helps reduce the time taken to complete them. It also provides better control of the overall close timelines, even when re-processing may be necessary.

1.3.3   Why use selection by segment in allocation cycles

The BASIS team at GCI performed detailed runtime analysis and recommended use of *selection by segment*.

Excerpt from the note: "In this method, the logic of the selection by cycle is performed for each segment. This means that the system determines

27

an interval of the cost centers for each segment and performs a database access using this interval. ...You should use this method in the following situations: if there is a manageable number of segments (up to 100) and if there are segment definitions that are far apart alphanumerically."

1.3.4 How to optimize the performance of allocation cycles

Transaction KSV5 is used to execute distribution cycles for actual costs, and KSU5 is used for assessment. As seen in Figure 1.7, clicking on the SETTINGS ⊞ Settings icon opens up another window. The field DATABASE SELECTION provides options for SELECTION BY CYCLE (default selection), OPTIMIZED SELECTION BY CYCLE, and SELECTION BY SEGMENT. Additionally, parallel processing can be used for the cycle to run on multiple servers, thereby improving the run time.

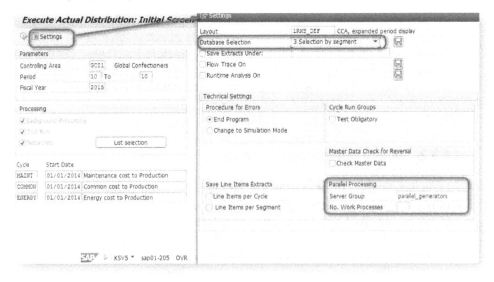

Figure 1.7: KSV5—Distribution settings: Selection by segment

The menu path to execute the distribution cycle is as follows: ACCOUNTING • CONTROLLING • COST CENTER ACCOUNTING • PERIOD-END CLOSING • SINGLE FUNCTIONS • ALLOCATIONS • KSV5—DISTRIBUTION

The menu path to execute the assessment cycle is as follows: ACCOUNTING • CONTROLLING • COST CENTER ACCOUNTING • PERIOD-END CLOSING • SINGLE FUNCTIONS • ALLOCATIONS • KSU5—ASSESSMENT

1.4   Expedite material ledger close

Knowing how much a product costs is essential to determining the actual profitability of a product. Yet most decisions are based on the standard cost of the product, given that it is not always easy to get an accurate picture of the actual cost. Actual costing functionality provided by the material ledger component of SAP Controlling bridges this gap. It provides the ability to capture actual costs by tracking variances at the material (product) level. This section provides an overview of actual costing in SAP Material Ledger.

"Alex, I remember you had mentioned that material ledger close takes a lot of system time. NCL's product volume is almost twice that of GCI. Do I need to worry about processing times in Material Ledger?" Frank asked.

"There is a function that will help expedite Material Ledger close; let me show you," Alex said.

1.4.1   What Material Ledger is

SAP *Material Ledger* inventory valuation includes the following:

- ▶ Collecting actual data during the month.
- ▶ Determining price: single-level and multi-level prices are determined based on the type of transactions performed.
- ▶ Calculating periodic unit prices at the end of the month.

SAP Material Ledger collects *material movement* data throughout the month and keeps track of which materials were used for the production of specific goods in production/process orders.

The SAP Materials Management module (in combination with the FI module) tracks goods movements and their values at standard cost, while the SAP Material Ledger tracks goods movement values at standard and actual costs. In other words, SAP Material Ledger can be considered a second set of books where each material has a record of all goods movements for actual valuation.

1.4.2   Material Ledger closing cockpit

The SAP Material Ledger closing cockpit is run every month to perform actual costing using transaction code CKMLCP. The menu path is as follows: ACCOUNTING • CONTROLLING • PRODUCT COST CONTROLLING • AC-TUAL COSTING/MATERIAL LEDGER • ACTUAL COSTING • CKMLCP—EDIT COSTING RUN.

The first step is to create a costing run and assign relevant plants.

After selecting plant(s), the Material Ledger closing cockpit requires several steps as shown in Figure 1.8

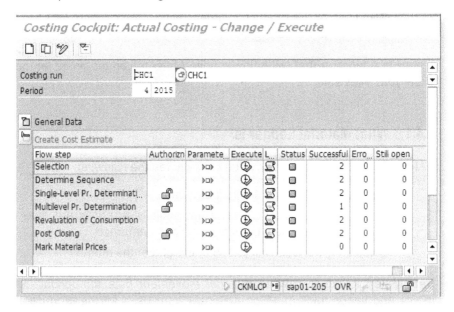

Figure 1.8: CKMLCP—SAP Material Ledger closing cockpit process steps

1. SELECTION: all materials for the given plants are selected.

2. SEQUENCE DETERMINATION: the sequence of costing is established, starting with the lowest level material and going all the way up to the highest-level material and goods movements.

3. SINGLE-LEVEL PRICE DETERMINATION: prices are calculated for each material.

4. MULTI-LEVEL PRICE DETERMINATION: prices are calculated for the entire production stream.

5. REVALUATION OF CONSUMPTION: adjustment posting of actual costs at month end, where all variances are transferred to the receiving object (which can be a material, cost center, internal order, GL Account, etc., depending on where the original consumption occurred).

6. POST-CLOSING: all calculations performed in prior steps are posted during this step.

   ▶ Multi-level price differences are transferred to the next level.

   ▶ Revaluation of consumption is posted to cost objects.

   ▶ Inventory is revalued in FI for the period being closed.

7. MARK MATERIAL PRICES: this step is optional. An organization may decide not to use the periodic unit price as a standard for the upcoming month. If so, this step is skipped, and the system uses the standard price for goods movements and revalues at the periodic unit price only at month-end.

1.4.3   Performance improvement with parallel processing

Large run times and low system performance may become the norm, given that Material Ledger processes large amounts of data in the closing cockpit. Parallel processing can be used to address this performance concern.

As shown in Figure 1.9, there is an option to run Material Ledger close steps on multiple servers at the same time.

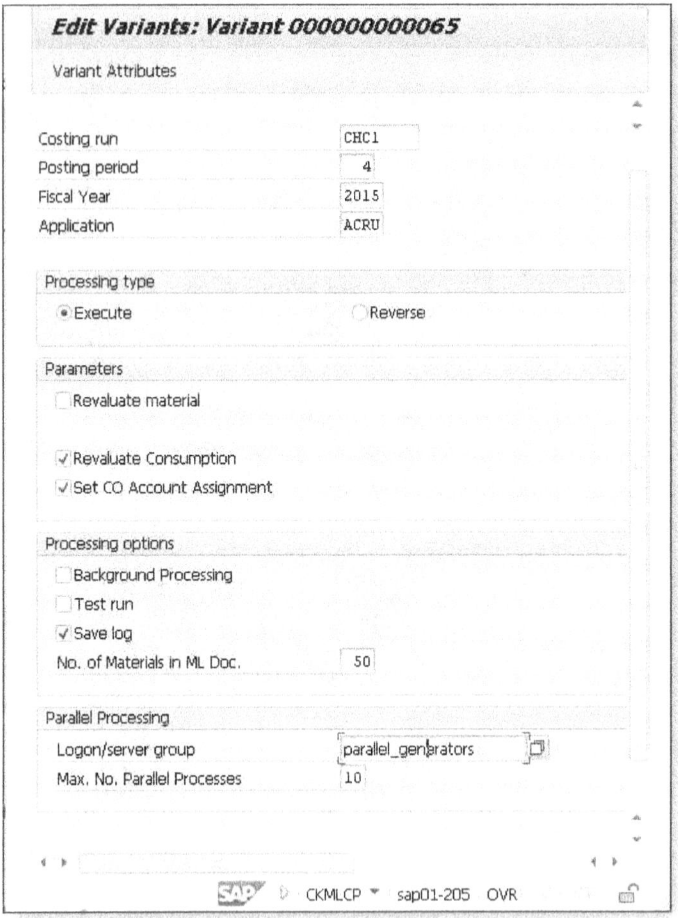

Edit Variants: Variant 000000000065

Variant Attributes

Costing run	CHC1
Posting period	4
Fiscal Year	2015
Application	ACRU

Processing type
- ◉ Execute
- ○ Reverse

Parameters
- ☐ Revaluate material

- ☑ Revaluate Consumption
- ☑ Set CO Account Assignment

Processing options
- ☐ Background Processing
- ☐ Test run
- ☑ Save log
- No. of Materials in ML Doc.   50

Parallel Processing
- Logon/server group   parallel_generators
- Max. No. Parallel Processes   10

SAP ▷ CKMLCP ▾ sap01-205 OVR

Figure 1.9: CKMLCP—ML Close: Parallel processing on multiple servers

This feature is often referred to as *parallel processing*. As seen at the bottom of the screen, SERVER GROUP "parallel_generators" has been selected, with the additional selection of MAXIMUM NUMBER OF PARALLEL PROCESSES as 10. This would mean that, instead of the usual single server, this job would be executed in parallel on 10 servers. This would imply that there would be an 85–90 percent performance improvement for this job.

Parallel processing setup requires collaboration with the BASIS team in your organization.

1.5 Utilizing cost center overhead charges

"My accounting team made the same error this month!" exclaimed Frank. "I wonder if we can automate the benefits accrual process so that we do not make mistakes."

"Yes, let's talk about this. I see this is an opportunity to improve," Alex said. He set up a conference call to discuss this with Erin.

"As we all know, our current benefits accrual process is very manual," Alex said during the conference call.

Business requirement:

▶ All organizations need to provide benefits to the employees, partly due to the legal requirements, and partly for retaining talent.

▶ Some organizations call it fringe benefits, some call it fringe, and some call it benefits.

▶ These benefits include contribution to 401(k) employee retirement plans, employee healthcare benefits, employee vacations, bonuses, holidays, and so on. These expenses are above the salary paid to the staff, but their actual payout may differ from month to month.

▶ We need to account for these benefits every month, based on certain pre-determined surcharge (or overhead) rates.

▶ The benefits surcharge usually is set during the annual budget process. The surcharge rate varies every year by country.

Current process at GCI:

▶ We download actual salary information by cost center using transaction KSB1.

▶ We then use a spreadsheet to apply a pre-determined percentage for benefits.

▶ Current year overhead rates are applied: 40 percent for US entities and 32 percent for Canadian entities.

▶ We use information from the spreadsheet to post an auto-reversing journal entry in the system for the benefits accrual amount.

- ▶ There are some manual steps, and if our accounting team is not careful, we may miss some cost centers in the download or may make mistakes in the spreadsheet that is used for posting the journal entry.
- ▶ Additionally, since there are different rates for different company codes, we may mix up the cost centers and rates and apply an incorrect rate if we are not careful.

"Exactly, that is my point," said Frank, who had been using the SAP system for about a year. "Since the salary data is already in the system, is there a way for us to apply the surcharge directly in the system? That way, we don't have to download this data, manipulate the numbers on a spreadsheet, and then post manually in the system."

"We can explore the *cost center overhead calculation* to meet this requirement," Erin said. "If I have understood this correctly, it sounds like this is a monthly process, and rates vary every year. You are looking for the post-overhead surcharge on the cost centers where the actual salary was paid. Is that correct?"

"Absolutely!" Alex and Frank responded almost at the same time.

"Ok, great. Therefore, it is clear that you are charging individual cost centers for the benefits overhead. One related question: Are you using a fixed cost center as a credit in the accrual journal entry?"

"Yes, we have one clearing cost center for each company code. This cost center gets debits occasionally when the actual payment is made. The accrual amounts are credited each month-end. Any difference is considered as over/under absorption and is used to set the overhead rate for the next year." Alex responded.

"Beautiful! Then I think I know the solution to this requirement. We will set up a costing sheet for benefits accrual and attach it to cost centers as a one-time effort. Your team will need to run transaction KSI4 for cost center overhead calculations. Once a year, the overhead rates will need to be updated."

"This is great, Erin! I am eager to see a prototype of this solution so that we can decide the next steps," Alex said.

"Impressive indeed; thank you, Erin!" Frank said.

"Sure, I will set up the prototype and list down the steps that are necessary to make this happen."

1.5.1 Cost center overhead calculation: One-time setup

Secondary cost element for accrual overhead calculation

▶ KA06—Secondary Cost Element 640000 (Benefits Accrual Overhead) should be set up (category 41). The cost element master data maintainer performs this task. Figure 1.10 has an example of cost element setup.

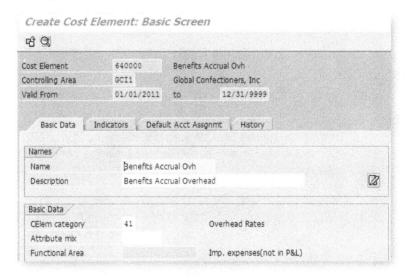

Figure 1.10: KA06—Create cost element for benefits accrual

Costing sheet setup with cost elements as base, percentage overhead rate, cost center for credit

▶ KAH1—Cost Element Group BENEF_CA (Benefits Accrual Canada) and BENEF_US should be set up with relevant cost elements used for the basis of calculation—this can be modified to additional cost elements if necessary). Figure 1.11 displays the cost element group for Canada.

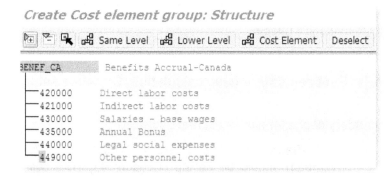

Figure 1.11: KAH1—Cost element group for benefits accrual

▶ KZB2—Calculation base Z100 (Benefits Accrual-US) and Z200 (Benefits Accrual-CA) should be set up.

Figure 1.12 displays the configuration setup for the calculation base.

Figure 1.13 shows the cost element group assignment to the calculation base.

This setup implies that all the cost elements that are included in this cost element group will be used as the base for overhead calculation.

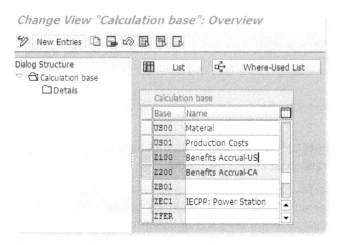

Figure 1.12: KZB2—Calculation base for overheads

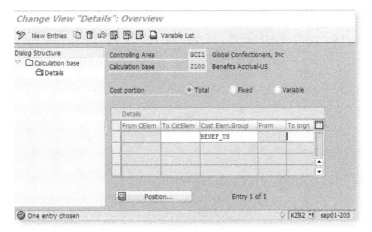

Figure 1.13: KZB2—Cost element group for calculation base

▶ KZZ2—Percentage overhead ZB10 (Benefits Accrual-US) and ZB20 (Benefits Accrual-CA) with the dependency D000 (Overhead Type)

Figure 1.14 displays the percentage overhead setup.

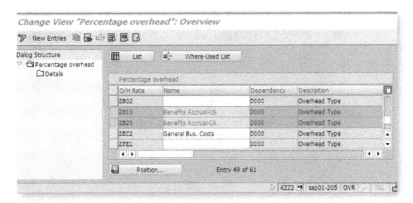

Figure 1.14: KZZ2—Benefits accrual—define percentage overheads

Figure 1.15 displays the percentage overhead for ZB10.

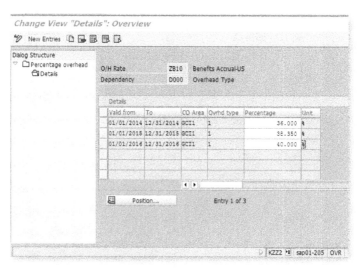

Figure 1.15: KZZ2—Benefits accrual—percentage overheads

▶ KZE2—Credit ZB1and ZB2 were set up (see Figure 1.16).

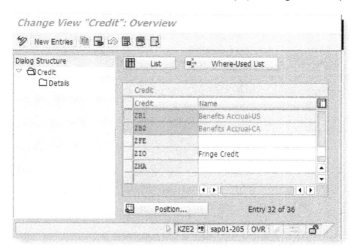

Figure 1.16: KZE2—Define credit key for overheads

Figure 1.17: Shows a credit to cost 640000, Cost Center C51900.

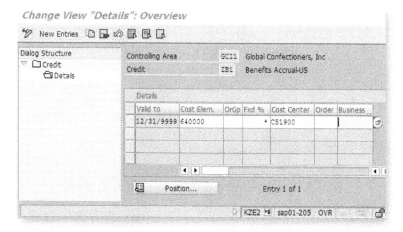

Figure 1.17:KZE2—Define details of credit key for overheads

▶ KZS2—Costing Sheets ZBEN01 and ZBEN02 were set up (Figure 1.18).

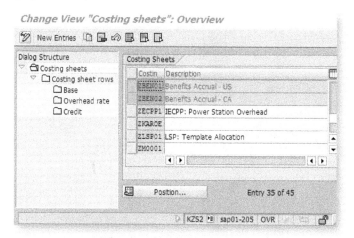

Figure 1.18: KZS2—Costing sheet setup

Figure 1.19 shows costing sheet rows where Z100 was set up as the base, ZB10 as the overhead rate, and ZB1 as the credit key.

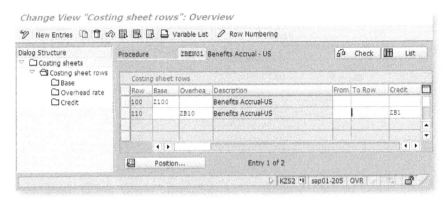

Figure 1.19: Costing sheet rows setup

Attach costing sheet to cost centers

▶ KS02—Cost centers should be updated with costing sheet ZBEN01 or ZBEN02 (for US/Canada). See Figure 1.20.

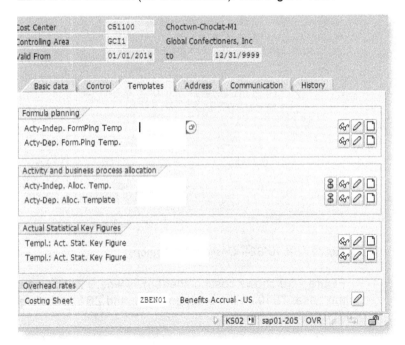

Figure 1.20: KS02—Cost center change, update costing sheet

▶ 0KM1—New screen variant with costing sheet was set up, and KS12 mass change can be applied (see Figure 1.21).

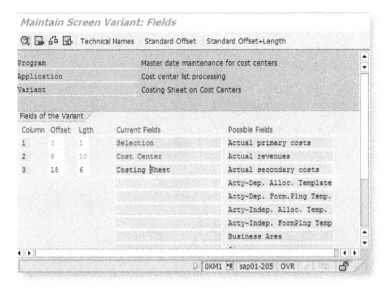

Figure 1.21: 0KM1—Screen variant for cost centers

▶ KS12—Cost center mass change (Figure 1.22, Figure 1.23).

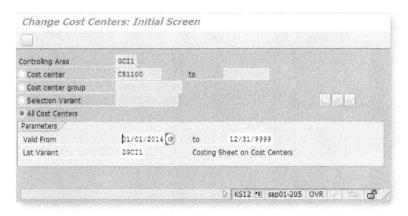

Figure 1.22: KS12—Cost center mass change—initial screen

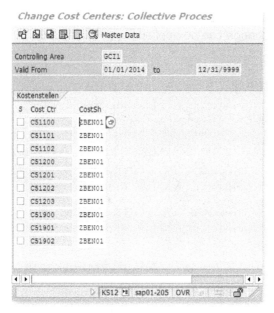

Figure 1.23: KS12—Cost center mass change—output screen

1.5.2   Cost center overhead calculation: monthly process

▶   Run actual overhead calculation using transaction KSI4 (see Figure 1.24 and Figure 1.25).

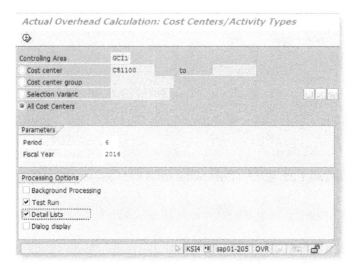

Figure 1.24: KSI4—Actual overhead calculation—initial screen

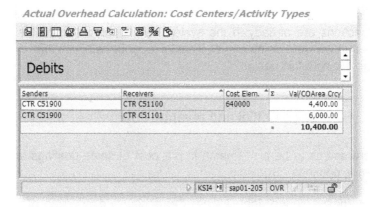

Figure 1.25: KSI4—Actual overhead calculation—output screen

► Validate documents and reports at cost center and FI-GL level (see Figure 1.26).

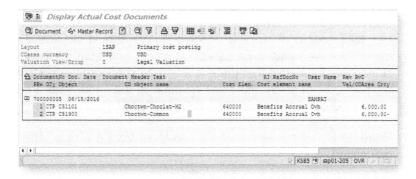

Figure 1.26: KSB5—Controlling document, cost center overhead

1.5.3 Cost center overhead calculation: ongoing maintenance

► Maintenance of benefits rate as it changes (KZS2)
► Maintenance of cost centers (add/change/delete) KS02/KS12

"So, what do you guys think of the new process?" Erin sought feedback from Alex and Frank.

"Looks promising!" Alex said.

"I agree, even though there is a lot of setup on the IT side, the setup for business is not much," Frank said. "You can run the transaction at the end of the month, validate the entries, and be done with it. Since the transactions are already in the system, we are avoiding all the manual work that we were doing earlier. Thanks for your help with this. When can we go live with this design?"

1.6   Harmonize COGS and revenue flow

"There seems to be a mismatch in our cost of sales postings and sales revenue postings," Bob said.

"That doesn't sound right. As per the accounting principle of matching revenues to costs, these two must match. What am I missing?" Alex responded.

"You're correct. If we have shipped goods, then we must post the sales invoice at the same time," Bob explained. "What I was told by the headquarters is that, at times, if there is an error in generating the invoice, it can take couple of days to resolve it. We should be fine during the month, but we need to be careful at month-end from the period cut-off standpoint. I was told that there is a way to configure the system so that we post cost of sales and sales revenue at the same time. I need your help in exploring this possibility," Bob concluded.

"Sure, Bob. Let me see what we can learn from this requirement," Alex responded.

After a few days of research and discussion with Erin and the others, Alex submitted a recommendation document to Bob. The document contained systematic procedures to implement this new design.

Current setup for post goods issue and sales invoice

The issue does not seem to be as much with the current setup, but more with the manner in which many open deliveries need to be invoiced at month-end. Transaction VFX3 (Release Billing Documents for Accounting) is being monitored regularly, but this list is not cleared at month-end. Due to this, there is a mismatch in the cost of sales (posted at the time of post goods issue) and sales (posted at the time of sales invoice)

▶ Post goods issue:

Debit   892000   Cost of sales—finished products

Credit   792000   Finished goods inventory

▶ Sales invoice

Debit   CCCC   Customer

Credit   800000   Sales revenues finished goods

Proposed setup for post goods issue and sales invoice

To overcome this timing noise of delivery and invoice, a new balance sheet account called "Shipped but not invoiced" is proposed. This account will replace the cost of sales account at the time of post goods issue.

▶ Post goods issue:

Debit   792001   FG Inv-Shipped, but not invoiced

Credit   792000   Finished goods inventory

Additionally, two additional account keys in SD-FI account determination will be introduced, which will post two additional lines on the sales invoice. One of the account keys will map to the cost of sales, and another will map to the new balance sheet account for shipped but not invoiced.

▶ Sales invoice

Debit   CCCC   Customer

Credit   800000   Sales revenues finished goods

Debit   892000   Cost of sales—finished products

Credit   792001   FG Inv-Shipped, but not invoiced

Until the all the deliveries are invoiced (essentially, VFX3 is clear), the balance in the new account is zero. However, if there is any balance in this account, then it is due to invoices stuck in VFX3.

Highlights of the proposed solution:

- ▶ Accounting at PGI will remove the cost of sales account and will introduce a new balance sheet account.
- ▶ Accounting at sales invoice will now have cost of sales, and the offset will be in the balance sheet account posted at the PGI stage.
- ▶ Balance in the new GL Account will represent "Shipped but not invoiced."
- ▶ All this is met with standard SAP setup—the change is performed in OBYC Account determination and VKOA SD-FI Account determination.
- ▶ This change will comply with the accounting principle of matching costs to revenue by posting sales revenue and cost of sales at the same time.

Changes necessary to implement this design

The below changes will be required:

- ▶ FS00 GL Account setup—Create GL Account 792001 "Shipped but not invoiced"
  - ▶ 792001 should be an exact copy of 792000, including an auto-post indicator
  - ▶ Use Field Status Group G030 (change in stock accounts)—the same as used for GL 892000
  - ▶ Ensure "Open Item Management" is activated
  - ▶ Sort Key Z00 "Material" should be created in OB16 and assigned in GL Account master
- ▶ OBYC MM-FI account determination—modify GBB VAX—replace 892000 (Cost of sales) with 792001 (Shipped but not invoiced)
- ▶ Current setup for GBB-VAX (varies by valuation class)
  - ▶ 892000   Cost of sales—finished products
- ▶ OV34 Define account keys
  - ▶ ZVP   Cost of sales
  - ▶ ZVQ   Shipped, not Inv;COS
- ▶ V/06 Pricing condition "VPRS" is flagged as an "accrual" account

- ▶ V/08 SD Pricing Procedure RVAA01—maintain account keys for VPRS—ZVP and ZVQ
- ▶ VKOA—SD-FI Account Determination—maintain entries for new account keys
    - ▶ Acct Key   GL   Provision Account
    - ▶ ZVP   Cost of Sales   <blank>
    - ▶ ZVQ   Shipped,   Cost of sales
                    not invoiced
    - ▶ Acct Key   GL   Provision Account
    - ▶ ZVP   892000   <blank>
    - ▶ ZVQ   792001   892000
- ▶ Review the configuration for "Classify G/L Accounts for document splitting" in the general ledger. The current range of accounts may need to be modified to accommodate 792001 and 892000 that were mapped to allowed item categories used for Document Type "RV" at the time of the sales invoice.

"This looks like a significant amount of work on the sales side," Bob said. "Do you think this will be an easy solution to implement? Are there any red flags or cutover considerations?" Bob asked.

"I learned from Erin that this design uses all standard SAP configurations. A lot of our sales team members have implemented a similar solution at other SAP installations and were glad to see that we are thinking of moving towards this setup," Alex responded. "I have also listed cutover considerations for your review."

Cutover considerations:

- ▶ All changes should be transported in one set.
- ▶ All pending deliveries should be invoiced before cutover.
- ▶ Billing blocked list should be cleared.
- ▶ F.13 Clearing (program SAPF124) should be established to run for GL Account 792001 in the background on a nightly basis.

"Of course, there is no guarantee that the mismatch issues will go away with this design. A lot of process improvement is necessary to strive for a zero balance in the new account. However, implementing this solution will help in identifying what deliveries are /pending in VFX3," Alex said.

"I agree; a lot of our problems start with an incorrect process. I am glad that we will now have a tool to highlight the lapses in this process. Thanks for your help with this," Bob concluded.

1.7 Maintain GR/IR Account periodically

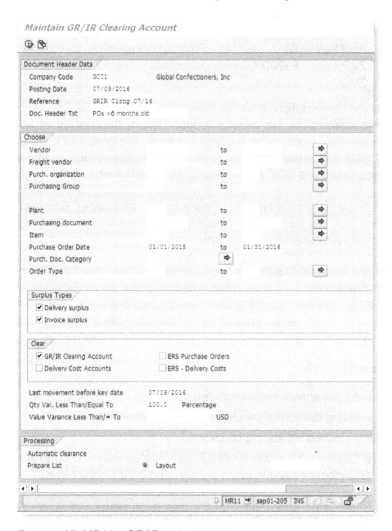

Figure 1.27: MR11—GR/IR maintenance

"We have some old purchase orders which are still showing up in GR/IR Account," Frank wrote in an email to Alex. "Some of them are minor differences for which the vendor would not submit an invoice. How do we clear such purchase orders?"

"I know exactly what you are talking about!" Alex responded. "We had the same issue here in Chocotown, and we were asked to use transaction MR11—*Maintain GR/IR Clearing* account."

Figure 1.27 shows the MR11 selection screen. Purchase orders older than six months are being selected for clearing. This is to allow invoices to be processed and posted in the system.

The menu path for MR11 is as follows: LOGISTICS • MATERIALS MANAGE-MENT • LOGISTICS INVOICE VERIFICATION • GR/IR ACCOUNT MAINTENANCE • MR11—MAINTAIN GR/IR CLEARING ACCOUNT

MR11 lists all the open purchase orders that fall into one or more of the following situations:

- ► Goods and invoices were both received, but there was a mismatch in quantity. Minor mismatches can be cleared directly using MR11. In fact, clearing minor differences (like short receipt, invoice differences within tolerances) is the primary use of MR11.
- ► Goods were received, but an invoice was not received from the vendor. Such instances usually require follow-up with the vendor. Even after a lot of follow-ups do not yield any result, then MR11 can be used to clear the old balance in GR/IR account
- ► Goods were returned to the vendor, but there was no credit note received or posted in the system. Such instances may also require follow-up with the vendor for issue of credit note. MR11 should be used as a last resort.

The process flow for procurement transactions is given below. Observe the accounting entries at each stage, especially from the GR/IR Account standpoint.

- ► Purchase requisition (no accounting posting at this stage)
- ► Purchase order (no accounting posting at this stage)
- ► Goods receipt:
  - ► Debit inventory
  - ► Credit GR/IR
  - ► Debit/credit purchase price variance (PPV)

- ▶ Invoice receipt
  - ▶ Debit GR/IR
  - ▶ Credit vendor
  - ▶ Debit/credit PPV
- ▶ Outgoing payment
  - ▶ Debit vendor
  - ▶ Credit bank

If we take the scenario where goods were received but an invoice was not received, clearing the entire difference using MR11 will post the following entry:

- ▶ Debit GR/IR
- ▶ Credit PPV

Essentially, the system is writing off the liability and reclassifying it on the income statement under the purchase price variance (PPV) account. This can create wide swings on the profitability numbers for the business. MR11 postings therefore need to have prior approval. MR11 gives an option to PREPARE LIST, WHICH provides a list of purchase orders that need to be cleared and the financial impact if the difference was cleared. This list can be a good starting point for seeking approvals from the finance leadership.

Documents posted using MR11 can be reviewed using transaction MR11SHOW.

The menu path for MR11 is as follows: LOGISTICS • MATERIALS MANAGEMENT • LOGISTICS INVOICE VERIFICATION • GR/IR ACCOUNT MAINTENANCE • MR11SHOW—DISPLAY/CANCEL ACCOUNT MAINTENANCE DOCUMENT

"Thanks, Alex. Your email was very helpful. I will ask my team to review the documents in MR11 in test mode before they post them," Frank said.

2 Transaction processing tips

This chapter covers SAP Controlling transaction processing tips that will assist with efficient and accurate transaction data capture.

If we were to visualize organization structure, master data, and transaction data in a pyramid form, organization structure sits at the top of the pyramid, the master data layer is at the center of the pyramid, and the transaction processing layer is at the bottom of the pyramid. Master data inherits a lot of organization structure information and passes it along to the transaction processing layer.

Accurate maintenance of master data is important to ensure consistent capture of data on the transaction processing layer.

2.1 Capture Trading Partner on transactions

Trading Partner is a term used in trade and commerce and can be generally defined as "one of the two or more participants in an ongoing business relationship."

Trading Partner has a similar meaning in the context of SAP Finance and Controlling; it speaks about the business relationship among company codes (generally referred to as intercompany postings). The requirement is to capture Trading Partner (field VBUND) at the relevant master data and transactional data. This data can then be used to consolidate financial statements as well as reporting.

"Given that we have a lot of intercompany transactions between NCL and GCI, we would like to enforce a system check to ensure Trading Partner is accurately captured," Bob explained to Alex. "Can you work with Erin to explore what options do we have to achieve this?"

"Yes, this was one of the concerns I had as well. I am sure there is a way to implement a check; perhaps we can look at field status groups. I will check with Erin," Alex replied.

"Field status is actually not a full-proof option for Trading Partner," Erin told Alex that afternoon. "Let me explain why," she continued.

2.1.1   Trading Partner (Company) setup

The Trading Partner field is defined in the configuration node for "Company" (field RASSC).

- ▶ Transaction OX15—Define Company (updates table T880)
- ▶ Transaction OX16—Assign Company code to Company

Company is set up using configuration transaction OX15. SAP menu path for company setup: TOOLS • CUSTOMIZING • IMG • SPRO EXECUTE PROJECT • ENTERPRISE STRUCTURE • DEFINITION • FINANCIAL ACCOUNTING • OX15—DEFINE COMPANY

Company code is assigned to company using configuration transaction OX16. SAP menu path for company setup: TOOLS • CUSTOMIZING • IMG • SPRO EXECUTE PROJECT • ENTERPRISE STRUCTURE • ASSIGNMENT • FINANCIAL ACCOUNTING • OX16—ASSIGN COMPANY CODE TO COMPANY

2.1.2   Trading Partner maintenance in master data

Once Trading Partner is maintained in relevant intercompany customers, vendors and GL Accounts—its data flows automatically to the transactions.

- ▶ Transaction FK02—Vendor Master (updates table LFA1)
- ▶ Transaction FD02—Customer Master (updates table KNA1)
- ▶ Transaction FS00—GL Account Master Data (updates table SKA1)

However, there may be instances where a GL Account may have transactions for both intercompany as well as third party scenarios (e.g., interest on loans and advances). It may not always be possible to define separate GL Accounts for each scenario; doing so may lead to a proliferation of GL Accounts. Since the Trading Partner is not maintained on GL Account master data in such a situation, Trading Partner will need to be explicitly entered at the transaction processing level. It is possible that the Trading Partner will be missed on certain transactions, thereby leading to inconsistencies and downstream impact on consolidations.

2.1.3 Making Trading Partner a required entry

How can we make Trading Partner a required entry while posting financial accounting documents for certain GL Accounts?

There are three possible ways to do so:

Field Status Group

There is a general belief among the SAP community that the field status group can be used to make certain fields required, optional, display, or suppressed by using *field status definition* (many a times interchangeably referred as *field status group* or field status variant). However, not all fields are available in the field status group—Trading Partner is one such field that is not a part of the field status group.

Trading Partner (VBUND) can be enabled in Field Status Group by adding it in table TCOBF (Coding Block: Assignment of Modif and Field Names from COBL). With this change, field status groups can now be leveraged to influence Trading Partner (suppressed/required/optional). However, this option is not recommended by SAP. It may create inconsistencies while posting FI documents (SAP Note 1397715 "Adding VBUND to the coding block"2)

- ▶ Transaction OBC4—Field Status variants
- ▶ Transaction OB14—Field Status definition
- ▶ Transaction OB41—Field Status groups (Posting Key level)

Document Types

Document Types can be configured such that Trading Partner will be available for input. Following fields need to be activated in the Document Type setup. This setup will open up Trading Partner at the document level. However, it does not make Trading Partner a required entry.

- ▶ Transaction OBA7—Document Types (underlying table T003)
  - ▶ Partner company can be input (T003-XMGES)
  - ▶ Cross-company (T003-XGSUB)

FI Validation

FI *validation* can be used to prevent document postings where Trading Partner is missing for certain GL Accounts.

▶ Transaction OB28—Financial Accounting validation

The SAP menu path for validation setup in Financial Accounting is: TOOLS • CUSTOMIZING • IMG • SPRO EXECUTE PROJECT • FINANCIAL ACCOUNTING (NEW) • FINANCIAL ACCOUNTING GLOBAL SETTINGS (NEW) • TOOLS • VALIDATION/SUBSTITUTION • OB28—VALIDATION IN ACCOUNTING DOCUMENTS

A validation in FI has three sections: Prerequisite, Check, and Message. These sections are explained below with examples. *Sets* are maintained using transaction GS01.

The SAP menu path for setup of sets is: ACCOUNTING • CONTROLLING • COST ELEMENT ACCOUNTING • INFORMATION SYSTEM • TOOLS • REPORT PAINTER • REPORT WRITER • SET • GS01—CREATE

1. Prerequisite:

▶ For certain set of accounts (defined in set "ZGL_TRAD_PART_REQD"—Figure 2.1)

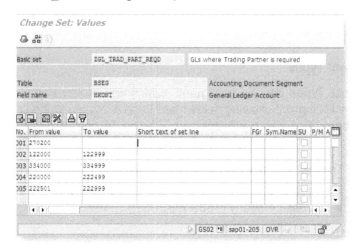

Figure 2.1: GS01/GS02—Create/Maintain set for GL Accounts checked for Trading Partner

▶ For certain sets of users (defined in set "ZUSR_TRAD_
PART_REQD"—Figure 2.2)

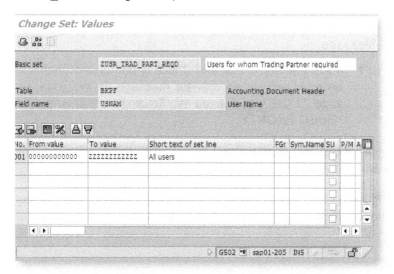

*Figure 2.2: GS01/GS02—Create/Maintain set for users checked for
Trading Partner*

▶ For certain document types (defined in set "ZDOC_TYPE_
TRAD_PART_REQD"—Figure 2.3)

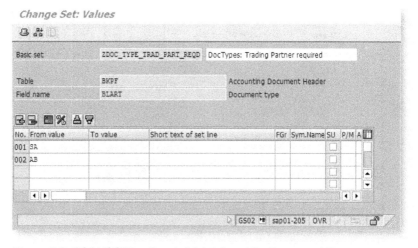

*Figure 2.3: GS01/GS02—Create/Maintain set for Document Types
checked for Trading Partner*

2. Check:

▸ If Trading Partner is blank

3. Message:

▸ If Prerequisite is met and Check is not fulfilled, then it will return an error with an appropriate message. In this case, error message Z1 032 was defined as, "Trading Partner is required for GL <BSEG-HKONT>"

Implication: User cannot move forward with this transaction until Trading Partner is entered.

Figure 2.4 has a snapshot of the validation step for the Trading Partner required field.

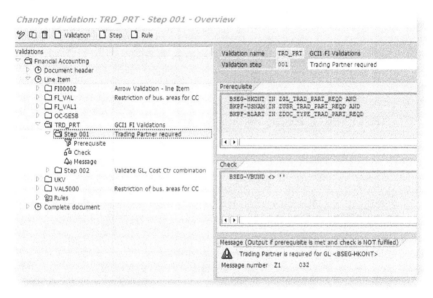

Figure 2.4: OB28: Trading Partner validation setup

Conclusion

Erin summarized her findings.

▸ Given the shortcomings of Field Status Group and Document Type options, these two options are generally not preferred.

▶ FI validations are easy to configure and maintain because they normally do not require ABAP programming unless a user-exit or table-lookup are to be used.

▶ A validation to ensure Trading Partner is entered in relevant intercompany transactions will go a long way in ensuring data consistency and accuracy for financial consolidation.

"That makes sense to me." Alex was happy to find a proven system solution that would work well for transactions between GCI and NCL.

2.2 Troubleshoot product costing messages

This section provides tips to troubleshoot common error messages encountered during costing in SAP Product Cost Planning (component CO-PC-PCP).

Product costs are impacted by multiple factors, including system design, accounting policies, business requirement, costing configuration and master data setup. It is therefore not possible to visualize and list out all possible errors during costing. This note covers the most common costing errors. An overview of cost estimates and costing run is provided as a background on this topic.

"We are doing our first mass costing, and these messages are driving my team crazy." Frank expressed his frustration.

"I can understand; it can be overwhelming at the beginning." Alex said. "Let me show you how to troubleshoot them."

2.2.1 Cost estimate

A *cost estimate* is the planned cost of a material or a production cost carrier. It utilizes the Bill of Material (BoM) and routing/recipe to arrive at the planned cost. This planned cost can be transferred to the material master, utilized in product costing to value the material.

Cost estimates are created using transaction CK11N (Create Material Cost Estimate with Quantity Structure). The menu path is as follows: CONTROLLING • PRODUCT COST CONTROLLING • PRODUCT COST PLANNING •

MATERIAL COSTING • COST ESTIMATE WITH QUANTITY STRUCTURE • CK11N—CREATE.

Once reviewed and validated for accuracy, cost estimates are *marked* and *released* using transaction CK24 (Price Update: Mark/Release Standard Price). Certain cost estimates can be created only for the purpose of analysis but need not be released as a standard cost estimate in the material master.

The menu path is as follows: CONTROLLING • PRODUCT COST CONTROLLING • PRODUCT COST PLANNING • MATERIAL COSTING • CK24—PRICE UPDATE.

2.2.2 Costing run

Mass costing, often referred to as *costing run,* is carried out using transaction CK40N (Edit Costing Run). The costing run enables the costing of multiple materials at the same time. A costing run reproduces the entire process of costing a product with a Bill of Material (BoM). Mainly suited to carry out costing for a large set of data, this can be executed in background mode for large volumes of materials.

Costing results can be used to mark and release several standard cost estimates at once. Mark and release steps are built into the CK40N mass costing run (unlike CK11N individual costing, where mark and release are performed using another transaction, CK24).

The menu path is as follows: CONTROLLING • PRODUCT COST CONTROLLING • PRODUCT COST PLANNING • MATERIAL COSTING • COSTING RUN • CK40N— EDIT COSTING RUN.

2.2.3 Steps in costing run

Costing run involves following steps:

- ▶ Selection—materials are selected for the given plant/co code/material/material type restriction
- ▶ Structure explosion—bills of materials are created, routing/recipes are expanded, costing levels are determined
- ▶ Costing—materials in the lowest level are costed first (e.g., raw materials), moving upward to the next level

▶ Analysis—comparison with material master, and expected revaluation is calculated

▶ Marking—the costing result is updated as the future planned price in material master

▶ Release—the costing result is updated as the current planned price in material master

An example of a costing run is provided in Figure 2.5. The costing step has two errors; the costing log needs to be reviewed to analyze the errors.

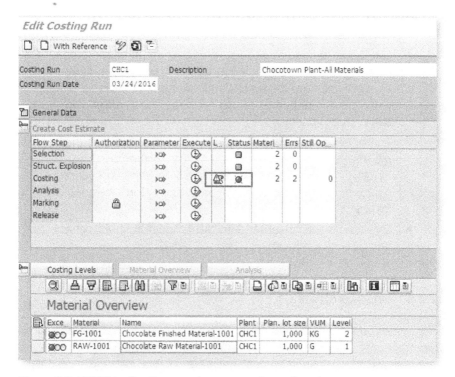

Figure 2.5: CK40N—Costing run steps, errors in costing step

There could be a situation in a typical SAP implementation project where master data has been set up for the first time. A wide open costing run of all materials may result in numerous errors and can make the error analysis and troubleshooting cumbersome. In this scenario, costing by costing levels is useful in segregating errors by costing level.

2.2.4   Costing drivers

Product costing is the valuation of material components and activities on a process or production order utilizing material prices and activity rates. Plan and actual values are recorded and reported with variances, and variances are disposed of according to company policy. Product costing is where all the direct costs for a product end up. From the perspective of inventory valuation, a manufacturing unit should include all the costs of raw materials and conversion costs, including any overhead that went into manufacturing a finished product. The following factors impact the cost of a product:

▶ Component material quantities are derived from a BoM.

▶ Components are costed as per costing method (standard or moving/weighted average), by reading the values stored in the material masters or purchasing information records (PIRs), or some other planned price valuation method like trending (historical average) price.

▶ The activities are costed by applying activity rates as the product moves through the routing (or recipe, in the case of a process industry) and operations performed in the work centers (resources, in the case of a process industry) in the manufacturing facility.

▶ Overheads are absorbed into the product cost via activity types and/or costing sheets.

2.2.5   Costing errors

Accurate and error-free costing is every controller's goal. Releasing an incorrect cost estimate may result in incorrect financial postings. It is not possible to release another cost estimate for the same period unless reorganization is performed. It is very important that a cost estimate be thoroughly reviewed before releasing the cost.

The costing run will be error-free when all the relevant master data is accurately set up. However, it is very rare that a costing run is successful on the first attempt. Getting all materials to cost successfully requires an iterative process where the errors are analyzed in detail, fixes are made, and costing is performed again. This cycle continues until the costing run is error-free AND the costing results are accurate and acceptable.

Figure 2.6 shows the contents of a log created at the costing step. Here are a few tips on how to review the log:

▶ Message type/traffic lights: Error messages are shown in red with message type "E." Information messages are shown in green with message type "I." Warning messages, if any, will be shown in yellow with message type "W."

All error messages must be resolved to mark and release cost estimates.

Information/Warning messages should not be ignored, as they may provide a hint to an underlying issue.

▶ There can be more than one error message for a given material and plant combination.

▶ Message class and message number are unique identifiers for each category of message, e.g.,

CK 240: "Cost component split costed with value of zero"—a generic information message applicable to both the materials RAW-1001 and FG-1001

CK 168: "Cost estimate for material RAW-1001/plant CHC1 is incorrect"—a specific message returned while costing material FG-1001

KL 023: "No control record for activity type GCI1 /C51100 /MCHRS in version 000/2016 activity planning/qty planning"— this message was returned twice for material FG-1001, for activities MCHRS and LABOR

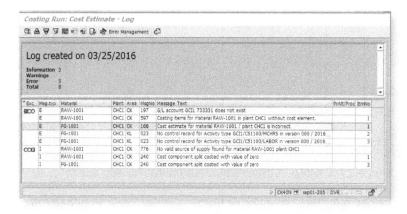

Figure 2.6: CK40N—Costing run message log

2.2.6 Costing errors by message category

Figure 2.7 contains a compilation of frequent messages seen during costing. Some of these messages can be cryptic and require further explanation and steps for correction.

Message Class	Message No.	Error description	Explanation / root cause	Steps for correction
KL	023	No control record for Activity type in activity planning / qty planning	Missing planning record for <CO Area>/<Cost Center>/<Activity Type> in <version> / <Year> combination	Maintain Cost Center Planning (KP26) for given combination in respective version and year
CK	060	Object was not costed	Missing procurement price / bill of material, depending on proc type (MM03-MRP2 view)	Maintain BOM if proc type in MM03-MRP2 "E" in-house production; maintain purchase price if "E" externally procured
CK	130	Work center <WW> in plant <PPPP> has no cost center	Material uses routing (CA03) that has work center (CR03) which is not assigned to a cost center	Maintain cost center assignment for work center (CR02) or Resource (CRC2)
MG	144	The field <MBEW-HRKFT> is defined as a required field; it does not contain an entry	Missing <Origin Group (field HRKFT)> in MM03-Costing 1 view	Maintain relevant views in material master (MM01 / MM02)
CK	168	Cost estimate for material <MMMMMMM> in plant <PPPP> is incorrect	Costing result of underlying material was incorrect cost rollup does not take place	Rectify errors in underlying materials
CK	197	G/L account <Chart of Account> <Account> does not exist	GL Account maintained in MM-FI Account determination is not setup (FS00)	Create the GL account, or modify GL Account in MM-FI Account determination (OBYC) for GBB-VBR
CK	229	No routing could be determined for material <MMMMMMM>	Missing routing (CA03) / recipe (C203) setup for the quantity structure date	Maintain routing (CR02) / Recipe (CRC2)
CK	239	Cost element <CCCCCCCC> is not assigned to a cost component	Missing assignment of cost element to cost components (OKTZ)	Maintain configuration for cost components (transaction OKTZ), map cost element to appropriate cost component
CK	240	Cost component split costed with value of zero	Costing result was zero, no cost components could be determined	Maintain BOM if proc type in MM03-MRP2 "E" in-house production; maintain purchase price if "E" externally procured
CK	322	Consumption account cannot be determined	Incorrect valuation class setup in MM03-Accounting 1 view	Check valuation class in MM03-Accounting 1 view/ A valid class will point to correct consumption account.

Figure 2.7: CK40N—Costing messages troubleshooting tips 1

Figure 2.8 contains more of the messages seen frequently during costing.

Message Class	Message No.	Error description	Explanation / root cause	Steps for correction
CK	323	There is no exchange rate for exchange rate type <P> on <MM/DD/YYYY>: <USD / EUR>	Missing exchange rate for currency combination for given exchange rate type and valuation date	Maintain exchange rate (transaction OB08, updates table TCURR)
CK	354	Material <MMMMMMM> in plant <PPPP> has material status 01 : Blocked for Procmnt/Whse	Material status does not require it to be costed	Change the status of the material (MM02-MRP1 view) or exclude the material from CK40N selection
CK	361	Value of costing item 00001 in itemization is 0	A component material in BOM has a zero cost (quantity and / or price are too small)	Analye data setup. Sometimes there could be valid reasons to have items on BOM with 0.001 quantity (CS03) or price at 0.01
CK	380	No valid source of supply could be found	Missing Source List (ME03)	Maintain Source List (ME01 or ME05)
CK	424	Material <MMMMMMM> plant <PPPP> has no BOM	Missing Bill of Material even though proc type (MM03-MRP2 view) is "E" In-House production	Create Bill of Material, or change the procurement type to "F" - External procurement
CK	465	No price could be determined for material/batch <MMMMMMM> plant <PPPP>	Costing result was zero	Maintain BOM if proc type in MM03-MRP2 "E" in-house production; maintain purchase price if "E" externally procured
CK	466	No price could be determined for internal activity <AAAAA> <CCCCCC>	Missing price for activity AAAAA and cost center CCCCC combination	Maintain activity price directly (KP26) or via activity price calculation (KSPI), verify price (KSBT)
CK	468	No price could be determined for subcontracting	Missing PIR (ME13) for subcontracting, even though MM03-MRP2 view has Special Proct Type 30 - Subcontracting	Maintain PIR (ME11 / ME12) with subcontracting category for the given valuation date
CK	597	Costing items for material <MMMMMMM> in plant <PPPP> without cost element.	GL Account maintained in configuration does not exist as a cost element (KA03)	Create the cost element, or modify GL Account in MM-FI Account determination (OBYC) for GBB-VBR
CK	776	No valid source of supply found for material <MMMMMMM> plant <PPPP>	Missing purchasing information record PIR (ME13)	Create PIR (ME11) or modify PIR (ME12) for the given valuation dates

Figure 2.8: CK40N—Costing messages troubleshooting tips 2

2.2.7   Transaction codes to troubleshoot costing messages

Figure 2.9 contains a list of transactions codes used to troubleshoot costing errors. Figure 2.10 contains transaction codes used for costing.

Category	Transaction description	Transaction code
Material	Display Material	MM03
Master	Material List	MM60
Bill of Material	Display Material BOM	CS03
	Explode BOM: Level by Level	CS11
	Explode BOM: Multilevel BOM	CS14
	Where-Used List: Material	CS15
Work Center /	Display Work Center	CR03
Resource	Display Resource	CRC3
	Work Center / Resource List	CR05
	Assignment of Work Centers / Resources to Cost Centers	CR06
Routing /	Display Routing	CA03
Recipe	Display Rate Routing	CA23
	Display Master Recipe	C203
	Production Version: Mass Processing	C223
Source List	Maintain Source List	ME01
	Display Source List	ME03
	Generate Source List	ME05
	Source List for Material	ME0M
Purchasing Information Record	Create Info Record	ME11
	Change Info Record	ME12
	Display Info Record	ME13
	Info Records per Material	ME1M
Cost Center Accounting Master Data	Display Cost Center	KS03
	Display Cost Element	KA03
	Display Activity Type	KL03
Cost Center Planning	Set Planner Profile	KP04
	Change Cost Element / Activity Input Planning	KP06
	Display Cost Element / Activity Input Planning	KP07
	Change Activity Type / Price Planning	KP26
	Display Activity Type / Price Planning	KP27
	Activity Type Price Report	KSBT

Figure 2.9: Transaction codes for troubleshooting costing errors

Category	Transaction description	Transaction code
Individual Costing	Create Material Cost Estimate with Quantity Structure	CK11N
	Display Material Cost Estimate with Quantity Structure	CK13N
	Price Update: Mark Standard Price	CK24
	Price Update: Release Standard Price	CK24
	Comparison of Itemization	CK33
	Display Price Change Document	CKMPCD
	Reorganization of Cost Estimates	CKR1
Mass Costing	Edit Costing Run	CK40N
	Delete Costing Run	CK44
	Display Materials To Be Costed	CKAPP01
	Search for Price Change Documents	CKMPCSEARCH
Reports	Analyze/Compare Material Cost Estimates: Results of Costing Run	S_ALR_87099930
	Analyze/Compare Material Cost Estimates: Price vs Cost Estimate	S_ALR_87099931
	Analyze/Compare Material Cost Estimates: Variances Between Costing Runs	S_ALR_87099932
	Analyze/Compare Material Cost Estimates: Cost Estimate List	S_P99_41000111

Figure 2.10: Transaction codes used for costing

2.3   Record GL Account consistently

This tip explains how to prevent GL Account overrides during inventory posting transactions

"I am analyzing scrap transactions, and I see that they booked over several GL Accounts." Frank was worried. "It's the same with samples. I was taught that one movement type is mapped to one GL Account, so why is it that I see the postings on different GL Accounts?"

"I understand your concern. You are correct in that one movement type should hit one GL Account. However, if the GL Account is available for entry at the time of a material movement transaction, it can potentially be overwritten. I suspect this is what is happening in your case," Alex explained.

Goods movements are typically performed using the MIGO transaction (or one of its variants, like MIGO_GI, MIGO_GR, MB1A, MB1C, MB11 and so on). Standard setup for movement type has the general ledger account as an optional field at the time of goods movement. The following situations may arise when the GL Account is an optional input field during goods movement:

▶ GL from OBYC account determination is used for posting if GL Account is left blank during MIGO posting.

▶ GL from OBYC account determination is not invoked if an explicit entry is made to GL Account.

The SAP menu path for MM-FI account determination configuration is: TOOLS • CUSTOMIZING • IMG • SPRO EXECUTE PROJECT • MATERIALS MANAGEMENT • VALUATION AND ACCOUNT ASSIGNMENT • ACCOUNT DETERMINATION • ACCOUNT DETERMINATION WITHOUT WIZARD • OMWB—CONFIGURE AUTOMATIC POSTINGS • OBYC—ACCOUNT ASSIGNMENT

As shown in Figure 2.11, the GL Account was available for input during scrap posting (movement type 551)—this is the default setup.

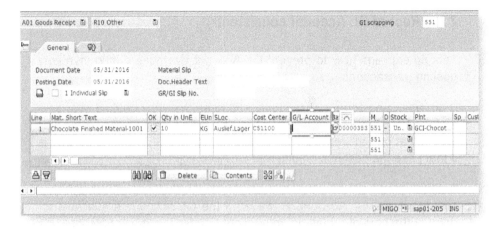

Figure 2.11: MIGO—GL Account available for input during scrap posting

Posting different accounts in different transactions for the same movement type can create inconsistencies and lead to incorrect accounting postings. Such a situation may translate into a requirement to ensure that manual account assignment is not allowed.

GL Account input can be controlled by the configuration transaction OMJJ. Two radio buttons ⊙ are available, Required Entry and Optional Entry. There is no separate radio button to suppress a specific field.

Combination of Movement Type and field KONTO (G/L Account) needs to be deleted from this configuration setup. Doing so will ensure GL Account is suppressed and not available for input in MIGO for that specific movement type.

As shown in Figure 2.12, field KONTO was removed for movement type 551 in transaction OMJJ.

The menu path for configuration transaction OMJJ is as follows: TOOLS • CUSTOMIZING • IMG • SPRO EXECUTE PROJECT • MATERIALS MANAGEMENT • INVENTORY MANAGEMENT AND PHYSICAL INVENTORY • MOVEMENT TYPES • OMJJ—COPY, CHANGE MOVEMENT TYPES.

Once the GL Account field is removed from the movement type configuration, future MIGO transactions will suppress GL Account at the transaction posting. As shown in Figure 2.13, GL Account was not available for input in MIGO.

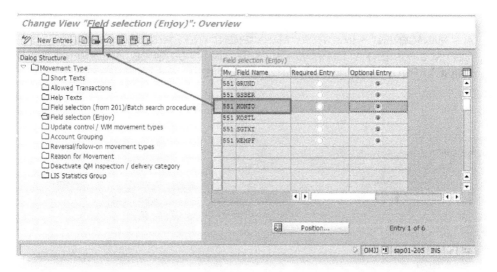

Figure 2.12: OMJJ—Remove GL Account from Field Selection in Movement Type

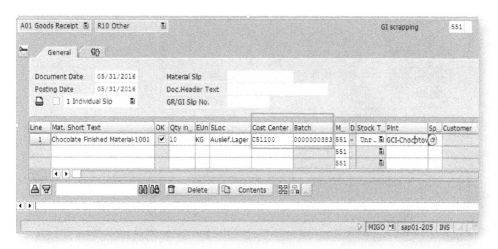

Figure 2.13: MIGO—GL Account suppressed during scrap posting

Similar action will need to be taken for other movement types to prevent manual override. This can be cumbersome if there are many movement types involved. Many goods movements can be addressed at once using the transaction illustrated in Figure 2.14.

TOOLS • CUSTOMIZING • IMG • SPRO EXECUTE PROJECT • SPRO • MATERI-
ALS MANAGEMENT • INVENTORY MANAGEMENT AND PHYSICAL INVENTORY •
SETTINGS FOR ENJOY TRANSACTIONS • SETTINGS FOR GOODS MOVEMENTS
(MIGO) • FIELD SELECTION PER MOVEMENT TYPE

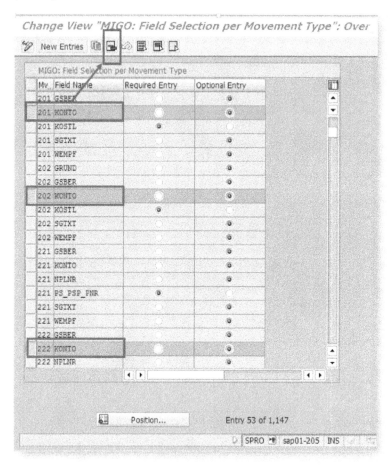

Figure 2.14: Remove GL Account from Field Selection for multiple movement
types

2.4   Prevent duplicate vendor invoices

"I can't believe this. How can the SAP system allow an invoice to be paid
twice? I didn't think this was possible." Frank's email had a worried tone.
"Please review the email thread below. My team found this issue during a
routine account statement check. It looks like a single goods receipt had

an invoice submitted against it. There was also an ERS posting. Both the invoices were paid. I am having my team create a debit note to the vendor to adjust future payments, so we are covered this time, but can you help me find the root cause and help implement additional controls?"

Alex went through the details of the email and realized what had happened. He sent additional details to Frank in his email explaining the scenario and how could this situation be avoided in the future.

Procurement (or purchasing) is one of the most important functions in an organization. This process encompasses the following steps.

2.4.1 Procure-to-pay process

- ▶ Purchase requisition (no accounting posting at this stage)
- ▶ Purchase order (no accounting posting at this stage)
- ▶ Goods receipt:
  - ▶ Debit Inventory
  - ▶ Credit GR/IR
  - ▶ Debit/Credit Purchase Price Variance (PPV)
- ▶ Invoice receipt
  - ▶ Debit GR/IR
  - ▶ Credit Vendor
  - ▶ Debit/Credit PPV
- ▶ Outgoing payment
  - ▶ Debit Vendor
  - ▶ Credit Bank

Vendors submit invoices in paper or electronic form. These invoices are typically posted using the MIRO transaction.

Various rules can be built to check for duplicate invoices, with the most commonly used rule being to check for the vendor invoice number, which is usually entered in the reference field. An example of these rules can be seen in Figure 2.15; these rules are set up in configuration transaction OMRDC for each company code.

The SAP menu path is: TOOLS • CUSTOMIZING • IMG • SPRO EXECUTE PROJECT • MATERIALS MANAGEMENT • LOGISTICS INVOICE VERIFICATION • INCOMING INVOICE • OMRDC—SET CHECK FOR DUPLICATE INVOICES

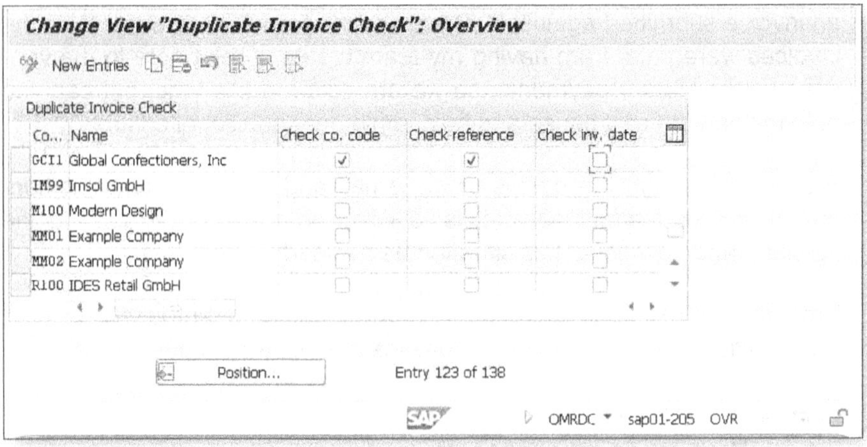

Figure 2.15: OMRDC—Configuration for duplicate invoice check

2.4.2   Evaluated Receipt Settlement

Evaluated Receipt Settlement (ERS) allows for processing of a vendor liability without the receipt of the actual invoice from the vendor. ERS is often used with vendors who have been consistent in providing goods or services. The SAP system posts the invoice document automatically based on the goods receipt. The transaction MRRL reviews goods receipts carried out for the given POs in the given period and automatically posts invoices.

It is possible that a vendor set up for ERS also submits an invoice. This could lead to a duplicate invoice posting. As shown in Figure 2.16, message M8-225 should be changed to an error message in transaction OMRM. This should prevent duplicate invoice posting via ERS (MRRL) and physical invoice (MIRO).

The SAP menu path is: TOOLS • CUSTOMIZING • IMG • SPRO EXECUTE PROJECT • MATERIALS MANAGEMENT • LOGISTICS INVOICE VERIFICATION • OMRM—DEFINE ATTRIBUTES OF SYSTEM MESSAGES

Error message M8 225: "Evaluated receipt settlement is active for purchase order XXXXXXXXXX" is returned when an invoice is entered using MIRO for a vendor who is set up with ERS.

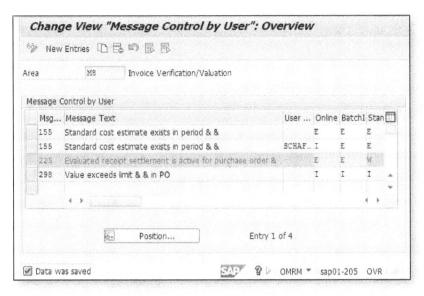

Figure 2.16: OMRM message M8-225 changed to error

2.5   Leverage CO validations

This tip will explain how to leverage validations in SAP Controlling using an example from maintenance department cost postings.

"Hey, Alex, the maintenance department has been complaining that there are a lot of postings to maintenance-related GL Accounts in the cost center, other than in the maintenance cost center. Is there any way we can always post maintenance postings to the maintenance cost center?" Carl asked.

"Sure, there is a way to prevent incorrect combinations of GL Account and Cost Centers. Let's discuss the right combinations, and then we can build a validation in Finance and/or Controlling," Alex responded.

"I would like to post these GL Accounts only to the maintenance cost center. That way we will be able to assess these costs accurately to all production line cost centers. If these GL Accounts post to other cost centers, I do not have a way to perform an accurate allocation," Carl said. "I am looking at the following GL Accounts to post only on cost center C51901 (Chocotown-Maintenance):

451000 Building maintenance costs

452000 Machinery & equipment maintenance costs

453000 Maintenance costs target=actual

459000 Other maintenance costs"

Validations contain user-defined prerequisite conditions that validate input values. Input value is transferred into the system if the conditions are fulfilled; otherwise, an error/warning message is issued. Validations are useful to ensure data consistency.

CO validations have three sections: Prerequisite, Check, and Message. These sections are explained below with examples. Sets are maintained using transaction GS01.

The SAP menu path for setting up sets is: ACCOUNTING • CONTROLLING • COST ELEMENT ACCOUNTING • INFORMATION SYSTEM • TOOLS • REPORT PAINTER • REPORT WRITER • SET • GS01—CREATE

1. Prerequisite: For certain sets of GL Accounts (defined in set "ZVALID_GL_LIST"—Figure 2.17)

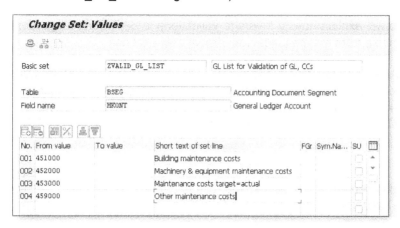

Figure 2.17: GS01/GS02—Create/maintain set for GL Accounts checked for cost centers

2. Check: For certain cost centers (defined in set "ZVALID_CC_LIST"— Figure 2.18)

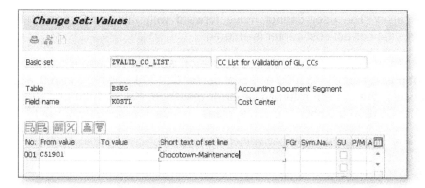

Figure 2.18: GS01/GS02—Create/maintain set for cost centers checked for GL Accounts

3. Message: If prerequisite is met and check is not fulfilled, then return an error with the appropriate message. In this case, error message Z1 033 was defined as "GL <COBL-HKONT> and Cost Center <COBL-KOSTL> are not compatible, please revise."

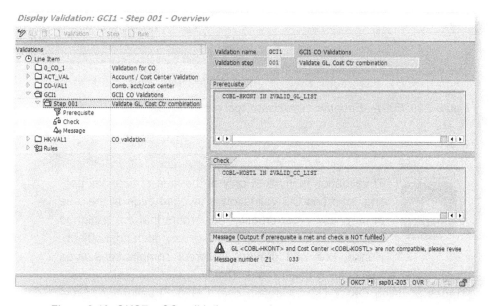

Figure 2.19: OKC7—CO validation example

Figure 2.19 provides a snapshot of this CO validation that was built in transaction OKC7. The menu path is as follows: TOOLS • CUSTOMIZING • IMG • SPRO EXECUTE PROJECT • CONTROLLING • GENERAL CONTROLLING • ACCOUNT ASSIGNMENT LOGIC • OKC7—DEFINE VALIDATION

Implication: The user cannot move forward with this transaction until correct the correct cost center is entered.

As seen in Figure 2.20, once the validation was set up, financial document posting for GL 451000 and cost center C51900 was not allowed. As expected, the system returned an error message, "GL 451000 and Cost Center C51900 are not compatible, please revise. Message no. Z1033."

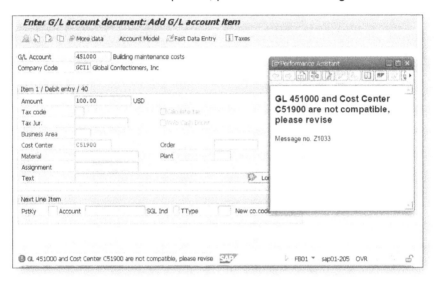

Figure 2.20: FB01—Error message invalid cost center on GL

When to use FI versus CO validation

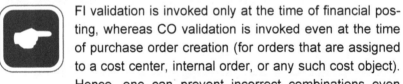 FI validation is invoked only at the time of financial posting, whereas CO validation is invoked even at the time of purchase order creation (for orders that are assigned to a cost center, internal order, or any such cost object). Hence, one can prevent incorrect combinations even before the actual posting takes place. This is one of the major advantages of using OKC7 CO validation over OB28 FI validation. However, not all postings flow to SAP Controlling when they are not created as cost elements. This is especially true in case of balance sheet accounts. FI validation is the only possible option when case balance sheet accounts are involved. One such validation is explained earlier in the book for Trading Partner on various P&L and balance sheet accounts.

2.6   Utilize user exit for material valuation

This tip will explain how to activate product costing user exits for material valuation.

User exit is standard SAP-delivered customization that can optionally be used to customize a different logic. It is a sort of minor deviation to the standard process.

"We want to use a forecast price for our procured materials next year. Can you find a way to use this forecasted price in standard costing?" Bob asked.

Alex responded, "There are many options available for costing: user of Purchasing Information Record (PIR); standard price; moving average price; planned price 1, 2, 3; commercial price 1, 2, 3; tax price 1, 2, 3 and so on. When none of these prices works for our design, we can activate a user exit. We can store the forecast price in a custom table and use this for valuation during costing."

"That is interesting!" Bob said. "I will get you the forecast prices from procurement team for each material. What else do we need to do this?"

"First, we will need to modify our valuation variant so that it looks for 'Valuation using user exit' (strategy U); if it does not find the price in forecast table, then it will use Planned Price 1 (strategy 4); finally, if either of these two are found, then price based on price control is used (strategy 7)," Alex explained.

Valuation variant defines how the material, activities, subcontractors, and overhead surcharges will be valued using strategy sequences for each, e.g., the first use 1, and if it has no value, use 2, and so on. The valuation variant is part of the costing variant.

The *costing variant* is a repository of certain business rules that contain all control parameters for costing, including parameters that control how cost estimates are executed and the material prices or activity prices that are used to value the costing items.

Figure 2.21 shows the VALUATION VARIANT configuration setup (transaction OKK4).

The menu path is as follows: TOOLS • CUSTOMIZING • IMG • SPRO EXE-CUTE PROJECT • CONTROLLING • PRODUCT COST CONTROLLING • PRODUCT COST PLANNING • MATERIAL COST ESTIMATE WITH QUANTITY STRUCTURE • COSTING VARIANT: COMPONENTS • OKK4—DEFINE VALUATION VARIANTS.

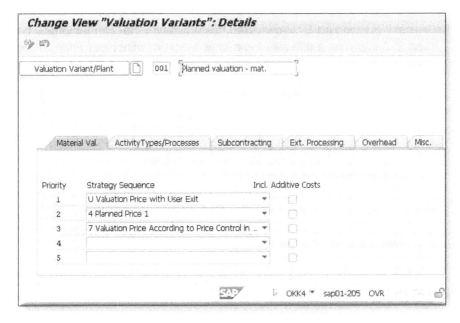

Figure 2.21: OKK4—Valuation variant—valuation price with user exit

"Next, we will activate user exit COPCP005 (User exit for material valua-tion [strategy U]) in transaction CMOD. User exit is standard SAP-delivered customization that can optionally be used to customize a differ-ent logic than what is standard. It is a minor deviation to the standard process.

"We will create a customized project ZCOPCP01 for GCI and assign enhancement COPCP005," Alex explained. See Figure 2.22.

The SAP Menu path is: TOOLS • CUSTOMIZING • IMG • SPRO • EXECUTE PROJECT • CONTROLLING • PRODUCT COST CONTROLLING • PRODUCT COST PLANNING • SELECTED FUNCTIONS IN MATERIAL COSTING • CMOD—DEVELOP ENHANCEMENTS FOR MATERIAL COSTING.

"This user exit contains function module, EXIT_SAPLCK21_002 (found in SE37—function builder), which has an include program, ZXCKAU08 (found in SE38—ABAP Editor). This include program will point to the forecast table," Alex concluded.

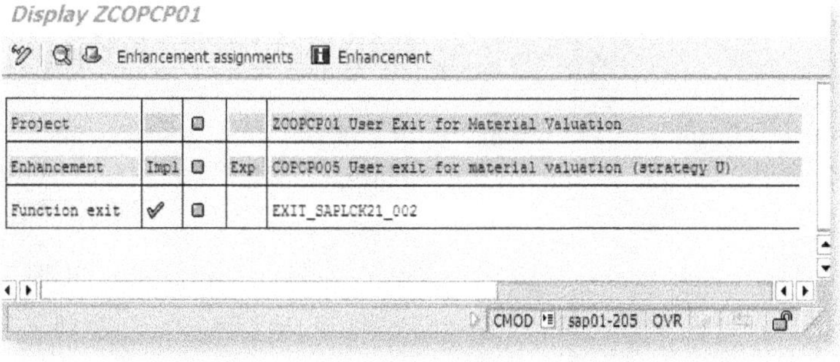

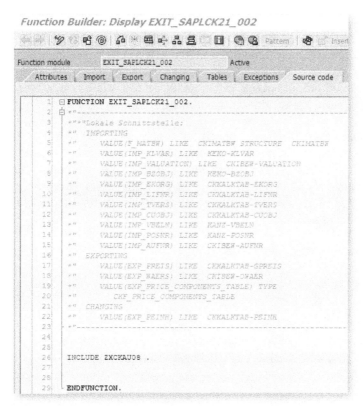

Figure 2.22: CMOD—Activate costing user exit COPCP005

Figure 2.23 shows the function module EXIT_SAPLCK21_002 and include ZXCKAU08.

Figure 2.23: SE37—Function module EXIT_SAPLCK21_002

The SAP Menu path for SE37—function builder is: TOOLS • ABAP WORK-BENCH • DEVELOPMENT • SE37—FUNCTION BUILDER

The SAP Menu path for SE38—ABAP Editor is: TOOLS • ABAP WORK-BENCH • DEVELOPMENT • SE38—ABAP EDITOR

"So, effectively, we are not deviating much from standard SAP; we are tweaking an available functionality somewhat to our advantage," Bob said.

"Absolutely!" Alex said. "Of course, this tweak is only applicable during the costing routine. It has limited use and should be used if none of the other options would work for us."

2.7   Discover subcontracting accounting

"Carl told me that we are unable to fulfill the increased demand that we have this holiday season," Bob informed Alex. "We are therefore exploring *subcontracted manufacturing*. As you know, we supply raw materials to the vendor and specify the quality guidelines with which the semi-finished or finished product needs to be manufactured. We pay a conversion fee/tolling fee to the vendor for this service." Bob said.

"I do know about the high-level process for subcontracting. We had it at my previous employer; it's just that we used to call it external manufacturing, or at times, third party manufacturing. It is a nice mechanism to address your capacity constraints. I don't have insight into the SAP setup for subcontracting, but I can do some more research with the help of Erin and others," Alex responded.

"That would be awesome!" exclaimed Bob.

Alex did some research and sent a document to Bob.

Configuration setup:

- ▶ The bulk of the configuration setup is on the purchasing side.
- ▶ One key feature needs to be activated on the finance side to ensure that price differences are correctly posted.

The menu path is as follows: TOOLS • CUSTOMIZING • IMG • SPRO EXE-
CUTE PROJECT • MATERIALS MANAGEMENT • INVENTORY MANAGEMENT AND
PHYSICAL INVENTORY • GOODS RECEIPT • PRICE DIFFERENCES FOR SUBCON-
TRACT ORDERS AT GOODS RECEIPT

Master data setup:

- ▶ Special Procurement Key in MRP2 view must be set as 30
- ▶ Procurement Type F is preferred and can set up X if the material is procured as well as produced
- ▶ Vendor code must exist for the subcontractor
- ▶ Contract must exist for the vendor and material combination
- ▶ Contract dates must be aligned with the valuation date used in costing run
- ▶ Source list dates must be aligned with the quantity structure date used in costing run
- ▶ Purchasing Information Record (PIR) with category subcontracting must be set up for the vendor, a purchase order must be created for the vendor
- ▶ A bill of material must be set up and pulled into the purchase order
- ▶ The purchase order should be set up with item category "L" (subcontracting)
- ▶ The date on the PIR must be must be aligned with the valuation date used in the costing run

Common errors during costing of subcontracted materials:

- ▶ No valid source of supply could be found—verify Source List validity date in ME01/ME03
- ▶ No price could be determined for subcontracting—verify PIR validity date in ME12/ME13
- ▶ Consumption Account cannot be determined—verify Valuation Class in MM02/MM03

Transaction flow for subcontracted materials:

- ▶ Transfer of raw materials from internal stock to stock at vendor
  - ▶ Transaction MB1B—transfer posting—is used to transfer stock
  - ▶ Special stock indicator "O" (stock at vendor) is used

- ▶ Movement type 541/541-O is used, there is no accounting entry at this stage
- ▶ Financial ownership of raw material stock still remains with us; goods are physically transferred to the vendor

▶ Production of semi-finished/finished material and consumption of raw material

- ▶ Transaction MIGO/MIGO_GR is used to record production
- ▶ Movement type 101 is used to record production
- ▶ Consumption of component materials is recorded using movement type 543-O
- ▶ Receipt of by-product is recorded using movement type 545-O
- ▶ Consumption can be recorded by accepting the default quantities pulled from the bill of material (commonly known as back flushing), or actual quantities consumed can be input, if available (commonly known as direct issue)

▶ Accounting entry for production/consumption will be as follows:

- ▶ Debit Inventory (standard cost of finished material)
- ▶ Credit GR/IR (tolling fee from purchase order)
- ▶ Debit Tolling fee (tolling fee from purchase order)
- ▶ Credit subcontract consumption (Cost of underlying component Materials consumed at the time of GR + cost of conversion fee for subcontractor)
- ▶ Debit/Credit Price Difference = Standard Cost of Finished Material—(Cost of underlying component materials consumed at the time of GR + cost of conversion fee for subcontractor)

▶ Subsequent adjustment for consumption of raw material

- ▶ Transaction MIGO_GS is used to record production
- ▶ No production is recorded
- ▶ Consumption of component materials is recorded using movement type 543-O/544-O

"Thanks for putting this together," Bob said to Alex. "This document is going to be very useful for initial setup, as well as for a training/reference document."

3 Key tips for configuration

This chapter covers key tips on configuration in SAP Controlling space.

SAP configuration refers to adapting the SAP software to your organization's needs. SAP configuration begins very early in the project phase and involves set up of client, organization structure, and rules around the maintenance of master data, as well as the capture of transaction data. A lot of the configuration setup depends on what design was adapted by the organization. Configuration is therefore the heart of an SAP project.

3.1 Display IMG Activity in SPRO

Erin forwarded an article to Alex and Frank. "Even though you do not get into customizing much, you may find this article interesting." Alex read the article.

Have you ever wondered, "What is the underlying transaction code for a specific configuration step?"

Have you ever had difficulty navigating through the customizing project to locate a specific configuration step and wondered, "Is there a quick way to enter a transaction code and get to the configuration step?"

You are not alone. In a world where every keystroke counts and every second is valuable, answers to these questions may be very helpful. Follow these simple steps to learn how to display IMG Activity. Transaction code is (generally) embedded in the IMG Activity. The last four characters (or letters) represent the transaction code.

Enter transaction code TOOLS • CUSTOMIZING • IMG • SPRO EXECUTE PROJECT • SAP REFERENCE IMG

From the menu path: ADDITIONAL INFORMATION • ADDITIONAL INFORMATION • DISPLAY KEY • IMG ACTIVITY (see Figure 3.1)

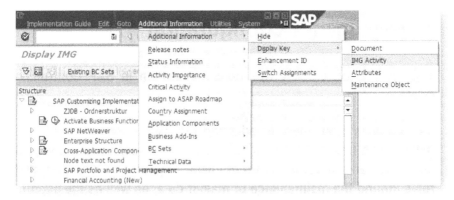

Figure 3.1: How to display IMG Activity in SPRO

For example, configuration step "Define Costing Variants" is attached to IMG Activity SIMG_CFMENUORKKOKKN.

This configuration step can be directly accessed from the command box using transaction code OKKN.

Figure 3.2 explains various examples of configuration nodes and their IMG Activity.

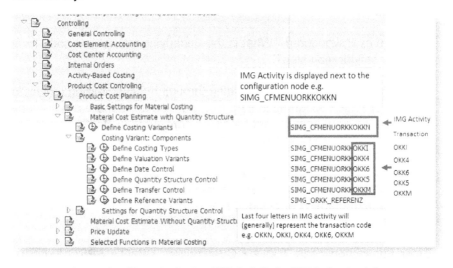

Figure 3.2: Example of how to display IMG Activity in SPRO Customizing

Almost all the configuration nodes have their own transactions. There are exceptions to this rule, though; IMG Activity SIMG_ORKK_REFERENZ for configuration node does not have a configuration transaction code embedded in it.

3.2 Evaluate the right cost object for you

"Erin, I remember you had explained difference between a process order and a production order, but do you know what a CO Production Order is? Are there any others that I should be aware of?" Alex asked Erin.

"Aside from Production Order and Process Order, there are many other cost objects available in the system," Erin responded.

"You are familiar with cost centers—they are another example of a cost object. Cost centers are not used in the manufacturing process, but more in overhead accounting," Erin continued.

Figure 3.3 depicts a tabular view of a cost objects comparison: prerequisites and setup.

Comparison of various cost objects used in Shop Floor Control and Overhead Cost Control

Process group	Process (rows), cost object (columns), transaction code (cells)	Production Order	Process Order	CO Production Order	Product Cost Collector	Internal Order	Plant Maintenance	Sales Order (as cost object)	Cost Center
Pre-requisite master data	Material Master	MM03	MM03	MM03	MM03	NA	NA	MM03	NA
	Bill of Material	CS03	CS03	NA	CS03	NA	NA	NA	NA
	Work Center / Resource	CR03	CRC3	NA	CR03	NA	CR03	NA	NA
	Routing / Master Recipe	CA03	C203	NA	CA03	NA	NA	NA	NA
Order / Object Type / Settlement info	Example Order Type (KOT2)	PP01	PI01	CP01	RM01	0100 / 0600	PM01	NA	NA
	Object Type (KOT2)	Production	Production	Production	Production	Overhead / investment	Overhead	NA	NA
	Order Category (KOT2)	10-PP Production Order	40-Process Order	4-CO Production Order	5-Product Cost Collector	1-Internal Order	30-Maintenance Order	NA	NA
	Settlement Profile (KOT2 / OKO7)	PP01-Production order	PI01-Process order	PP01-Production order	PP01-Production order	20-Overhead; 50-Asset Settlement	40-Maintenance	NA	NA
	Allocation Structure (OKO7 / OKO6)	A1-CO Allocation structure	A1-CO Allocation structure	A1-CO Allocation structure	A1-CO Allocation structure	20 - Internal Ord; 50 - Investmnt Ord	A1-CO Allocation structure	NA	NA
	PA Transfer Structure (OKO7 / KEI1)	E1-PA settlement	E1-PA settlement	E1-PA settlement	E1-PA settlement	E1-PA settlement; NA	NA	NA	NA

Figure 3.3: Cost objects comparison: Prerequisites and Setup

A *production order* is used to track *product cost by order* in discrete manufacturing and prerequisites from the master data point of view, including setup of material master, bill of material, work center, and routing. Order Type PP01 is used for creating production orders.

A *process order* is used to track product cost by order in process manu-facturing and prerequisites on the master data side, including include setup of material master, bill of material, resource, and master recipe. Order Type PI01 is used for creating production orders.

A *CO production order* can be used in any industry; prerequisites include setup of material master. Order Type CP01 is used for creating CO pro-duction orders.

A *product cost collector* is used in repetitive manufacturing to track *product costs by period*. A product cost collector is very much similar to a production order in terms of prerequisites: Material Master, Bill of Materi-al, Work Center, and Routing. Order Type RM01 is used for creating product cost collectors.

An *internal order* can be used to collect, monitor, and settle direct and indirect costs incurred by a specific project. They are cost objects that have a more dynamic nature than cost or profit centers. Logistics side master data is not necessary for the setup of internal orders. Several order types are available for use—depending on need and purpose (overhead of investment). Orders can be used as a primary cost object, which is then settled to a cost center or as a statistical posting object where the primary posting goes to the cost center.

A *plant maintenance order* is used to track costs related to planned or unplanned maintenance. It uses the work center as the primary master data element, apart from its own internal master data called functional location. Order type PM01 is used for creating plant maintenance orders.

A *sales order* is another type of cost object used to assign costs to a sales order. Whereas sales orders are primarily used in sales and distri-bution process in both made-to-stock and made-to-order scenarios, the use of sales order as a cost object part is mainly done in a made-to-order scenario.

A *cost center* is one of the most widely used master data elements in controlling. Cost centers allow departmental breakdown of costs. They are often the lowest level of an organization to collect and analyze costs and departmental performance. Cost centers are useful for the purpose of departmental budgets and plan versus actual comparison of expenses. Cost centers can also be used for the purpose of interdepartmental cost allocations through sender-receiver relationships.

"It sounds like we are not using many different cost objects here at GCI," Alex concluded.

"Which is ok; not all cost objects are relevant to us, and whichever one we are using meets our business requirement," Erin explained. "Carl mentioned the need to track maintenance costs, so Plant Maintenance may be the tool to use. However, such cost tracking comes with a lot of additional master data and transactional data to set up. So we need to decide if there is any value in implementing this tool in its entirety, or if should we simply track the costs in cost center."

"Can you explain what transactional setup will be required in each case so that we can determine if there is value in implementing these?" Alex asked.

"Of course, although these decisions need to be made by our leadership. I think these were reviewed during the implementation phase. Let's look at the benefits and costs associated with this," Erin said.

Comparison of various cost objects used in Shop Floor Control and Overhead Cost Control

Process group	Process (rows), cost object (columns), transaction code (cells)	Production Order	Process Order	CO Production Order	Product Cost Collector	Internal Order	Plant Maintenance	Sales Order (as cost object)	Cost Center
Cost object data	Create	CO01	COR1	KKF1	KKF6N / KKF6	KO01	IW31	VA01	KS01
	Change	CO02	COR2	KKF2	KKF6N / KKF7	KO02	IW32	VA02	KS02
	Display	CO03	COR3	KKF3	KKF6N / KKF8	KO03	IW33	VA03	KS03
Goods movement / activities	Goods issue	MIGO / MB1A	MIGO / MB1A	MIGO / MB1A	MFBF	MIGO / MB1A	MIGO / MB11	NA	MIGO / MB1A
	Confirmation	CO11N / CO15	COR6N / CORK	KB21N	MFBF	KB21N	IW41	NA	KB21N
	Goods Receipt	MIGO / MB31	MIGO / MB31	MIGO / MB31	MFBF	MIGO / MB31	MIGO / MB31	NA	NA
Period-end closing	Overhead - individual	KGI2	KGI2	KGI2	CO42	KGI2	KGI2	VA44	KSI4
	Overhead - collective	CO43	CO43	CO43	CO43	KGI4	KGI4	VA44	KSI4
	Revaluation of Activity prices- individual	MFN1	MFN1	MFN1	CON1	KON1	KON1	VAN1	NA
	Revaluation of Activity prices- collective	CON2	CON2	CON2	CON2	KON2	KON2	VAN1	NA
	Template Allocation - individual	CPTA	CPTA	CPTA	CPTE	CPTA	NA	CPTJ	KPAS
	Template Allocation - collective	CPTD	CPTD	CPTD	CPTD	CPTB	NA	CPTJ	KPAS
	WIP - individual	KKAX	KKAX	KKAS	KKAS	KKA1	KKA1	KKA3	NA
	WIP - individual display	KKAY	KKAY	KKAT	KKAT	NA	NA	KKA3	NA
	WIP - collective	KKAO	KKAO	KKAO	KKAO	KKAI	KKAI	KKAK	NA
	WIP - collective display	KKAQ	KKAQ	KKAQ	KKAQ	NA	NA	KKAK	NA
	Variance - individual	KKS2	KKS2	KKS6	KKS6	NA	NA	NA	KSS1
	Variance - collective	KKS1	KKS1	KKS5	KKS5	NA	NA	NA	KSS1
	Settlement - individual	KO88	KO88	KO88	KK87	KO88	KO88	VA88	NA
	Settlement - collective	CO88	CO88	CO88	CO88	KO8G	KO8G	VA88	NA
Reporting	Line Item Display (specific to object / generic)	KOB1	KOB1	KOB1	KRMI / KOB1	KOB1	KOB1	KVB1	KSB1
NA	= Not applicable								

Figure 3.4: Cost objects comparison: Transaction codes for various processes

Figure 3.4 depicts a tabular view of transaction codes for various processes across various cost objects.

▶ First, set up the prerequisites as shown in Figure 3.3.
▶ Once the prerequisites are complete, then transactional data for the respective cost object will need to be set up.

▸ Activity conformation and material movements (goods issue for consumption and goods receipt for production) are carried out using the individual transactions.

▸ Period-end transactions are performed. WIP, Variance, and Settlement are the most prominent steps; there may be additional steps around overhead calculation, template allocation, and revaluation of activity prices, depending on the business requirement and design.

"Nice! Thanks for your time in explaining the details of various cost objects. I will discuss with Bob to see if we can find value in using any of these functionalities that are not in use at GCI," Alex concluded.

3.3 Review Material Ledger configuration

Background on Material Ledger can be found in section 1.4 of this book.

"Erin, I learned from Bob and Frank that NCL is setting up a new plant in Candyville. Plant code CND1 and the related organization structure have been set up in test systems, and these are now ready to be migrated to production system. We do want to use Material Ledger in this new plant, just like how we have in our other plants. Can you advise regarding the steps required for setting up this plant on Material Ledger?" Alex emailed Erin.

"Sure. Since the basic design for Material Ledger was implemented a long time ago and has been tried and tested, we just need to extend this design to the new plant. We usually follow this checklist to ensure everything is set up correctly. Wherever you see our Chocotown plant CHC1, the same setup will be required for Candyville plant CND1," Erin explained.

▸ Activate Valuation Areas for Material Ledger
▸ Assign Material Ledger Types to Valuation Area
▸ Configure Dynamic Price Changes
▸ Activate Actual Costing
▸ Activate Actual Cost Component Split
▸ Assign Material Update Structure to Valuation Areas
▸ Production Startup of Material Ledger

"Interesting. Can you tell me more about these steps and how we would configure them?" Alex requested.

"Yes, I've included some steps below, and some screen shots," Erin replied.

► Activate valuation areas for Material Ledger

In this transaction, the valuation area (mapped to plant) is activated with Material Ledger. The plant code must be set up and assigned to the appropriate company code in order to perform this step. In the normal manufacturing operations where most materials are valued with a price control "S" (standard price), single-level/multi-level price determination is used. Materials such as plant maintenance that are generally valued with price control "V" (moving average price), do not have a requirement to roll up the differences in the next level material, and the transaction-based price determination is used. Figure 3.5 shows a snapshot of this configuration transaction.

This step is performed using transaction code OMX1 (IMG Activity SIMG_CFMENUOLMWOMX1). The SAP menu path is as follows: TOOLS • CUSTOMIZING • IMG • SPRO EXECUTE PROJECT • CONTROLLING • PRODUCT COST CONTROLLING • ACTUAL COSTING/MATERIAL LEDGER • OMX1— ACTIVATE VALUATION AREAS FOR MATERIAL LEDGER

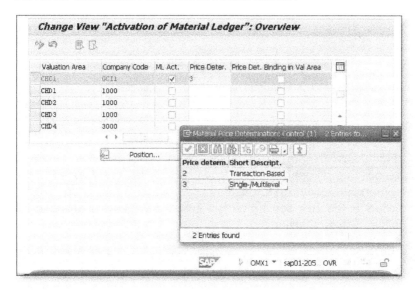

Figure 3.5: OMX1—Activate Valuation Areas for Material Ledger

▶ Assign Material Ledger Types to valuation area

In this transaction, valuation area (mapped to plant) is mapped to Material Ledger type. Material Ledger type is set up in OMX2 and determines the treatment of currencies between FI and CO. Figure 3.6 shows a snapshot of this configuration transaction.

This step is performed using transaction code OMX3 (IMG Activity SIMG_CFMENUOLMWOMX3). The SAP menu path is as follows: TOOLS • CUSTOMIZING • IMG • SPRO EXECUTE PROJECT • CONTROLLING • PRODUCT COST CONTROLLING • ACTUAL COSTING/MATERIAL LEDGER • OMX3—ASSIGN MATERIAL LEDGER TYPES TO VALUATION AREA

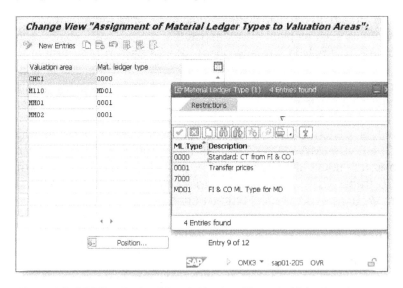

Figure 3.6: OMX3—Assign Material Ledger Types to Valuation Area

▶ Configure dynamic price changes

In this transaction, dynamic price release is set up for valuation area and its corresponding company code. *Dynamic price release* is used to release a marked standard price automatically when a first goods movement occurs in the new posting period. Figure 3.7 shows a snapshot of this configuration transaction.

Dynamic price change is configured using transaction code OMX5 (IMG Activity SIMG_CFMENUOLMWOMX5). The SAP menu path is as follows: TOOLS • CUSTOMIZING • IMG • SPRO EXECUTE PROJECT • CONTROL-

LING • PRODUCT COST CONTROLLING • ACTUAL COSTING/MATERIAL LEDGER •
OMX5—CONFIGURE DYNAMIC PRICE CHANGES

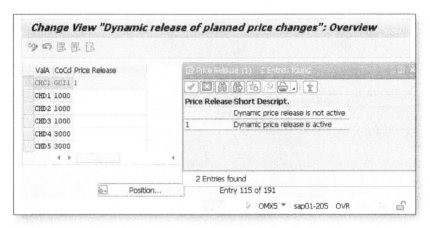

Figure 3.7: OMX5—Configure dynamic price changes

▶ Activate actual costing

Actual costing is activated for the given plant using this transaction. Additionally, the treatment of activity updates on price determination is configured. Figure 3.8 shows a snapshot of this configuration transaction.

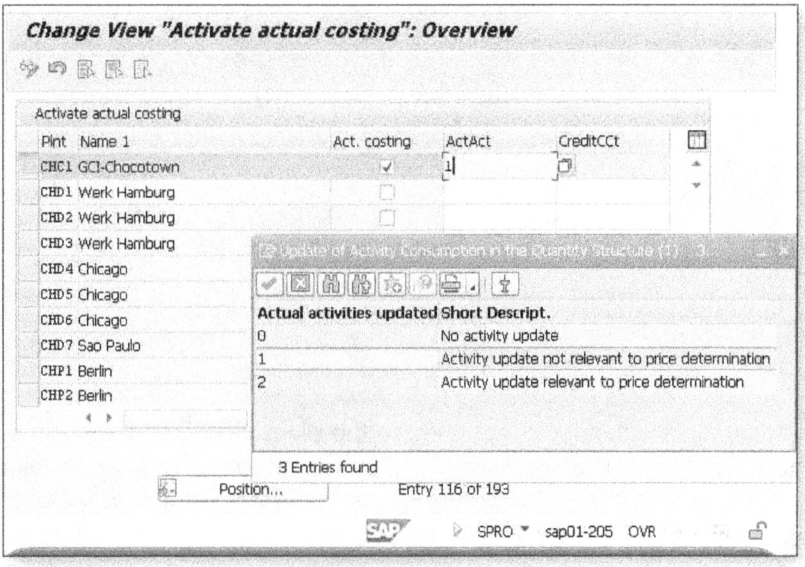

Figure 3.8: Activate actual costing

89

This step is performed using IMG Activity COPCACT_ACTIVATE. The SAP menu path is as follows: TOOLS • CUSTOMIZING • IMG • SPRO EXE-CUTE PROJECT • CONTROLLING • PRODUCT COST CONTROLLING • ACTUAL COSTING/MATERIAL LEDGER • ACTUAL COSTING • ACTIVATE ACTUAL COSTING

▶ Activate actual cost component split

Actual cost component split is activated for the given plant and company code combination using this transaction. Figure 3.9 shows a snapshot of this configuration transaction.

This step is performed using IMG Activity ACTCOSTCOMPSPLIT. The SAP menu path is as follows: TOOLS • CUSTOMIZING • IMG • SPRO EXE-CUTE PROJECT • CONTROLLING • PRODUCT COST CONTROLLING • ACTUAL COSTING/MATERIAL LEDGER • ACTUAL COSTING • ACTIVATE ACTUAL COST COMPONENT SPLIT

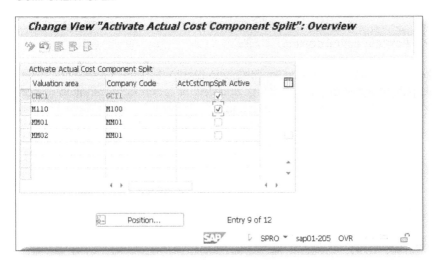

Figure 3.9: Activate actual cost component split

▶ Assign material update structure to valuation areas

Material update structure is assigned to the plant using this transaction. Material update structure is configured in transaction OMX9, along with its predecessor transactions Define Movement Type Groups of Material Ledger (OMX7) and Assign Movement Type Groups of Material Ledger (OMX0).

Figure 3.10 shows a snapshot of OMX8.

This step is performed using transaction code OMX8 (IMG Activity SIMG_CFMENUOLMWOMX8). The SAP menu path is as follows: TOOLS • CUSTOMIZING • IMG • SPRO EXECUTE PROJECT • CONTROLLING • PRODUCT COST CONTROLLING • ACTUAL COSTING/MATERIAL LEDGER • MATERIAL UP-DATE • OMX8—ASSIGN MATERIAL UPDATE STRUCTURE TO A VALUATION AREA

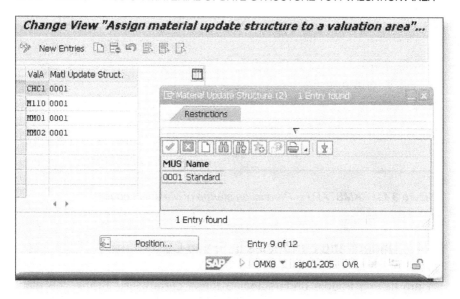

Figure 3.10: OMX8—Assign material update structure to valuation areas

▶ Production startup of material ledger

Once all the above steps are completed in configuration and moved across the landscape, transaction CKMSTART needs to be run to acti-vate Material Ledger in each of the target systems. CKMSTART is a pro-duction startup activity and is not migrated the same way configuration changes are migrated. Figure 3.11 shows a snapshot of CKMSTART.

The SAP menu path for CKMSTART is as follows:

ACCOUNTING • CONTROLLING • PRODUCT COST CONTROLLING • ACTUAL COSTING/MATERIAL LEDGER • ENVIRONMENT • PRODUCTION STARTUP • CKMSTART—SET VALUATION AREAS AS PRODUCTIVE

91

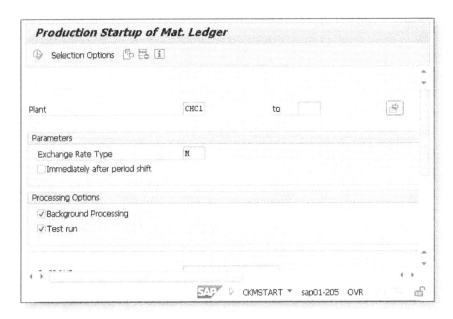

Figure 3.11: CKMSTART—Production startup of Material Ledger

3.4   Understand currencies in FI and CO

"I am having trouble understanding these currencies," Frank, the plant controller at NCL, said to Alex. NCL had been live on GCI's SAP system for two months. Frank was getting used to the system and wanted to call Alex to clarify his doubts.

"There are so many currency fields, so how do I ensure I am looking at the right currencies? In FI reports, I see the terms document currency, company code currency, and local currency 2. However, in CO, I see the terms transaction currency, object currency, and controlling area currency. In CO-PA, I find operating concern currency. Which one is which? I am confused," Frank explained to Alex.

"The terms may be a bit confusing, but they have a common link among them. Let me explain this to you with this small table that explains currencies at various places in FI and CO," Alex said. Figure 3.12 provides an overview of currencies in FI and CO.

Ledger / Module -->	Financial Accounting (FI)	Controlling (CO)	Controlling-Profitability Analaysis (CO-PA)	Material Ledger (ML)
Configuration Transaction	OB22 - Additional Local Currencies for Co Codes	OKKP - Maintain Controlling Area	KEA0 - CO-PA: Maintain Operating Concern	OMX2 - Define Material Ledger Type
Currency 1	1st Local Currency: 10 - Company Code Currency	10 - Company Code Currency	10 - Company Code Currency	10 - Company Code Currency
Currency 2	2nd Local Currency: 30 - Group Currency	30 - Group Currency	B0 - Operating Concern Currency	30 - Group Currency
Remarks	3rd Local Currency - not implemented in many instances	Checkbox "Diff Co Code Currency allowed"	Checkbox "Company Code Currency"	Checkbox "Currency Transfer from FI" i.e. inherits from OB22 setting in FI
Examples - Local	CCC = EUR, GBP, CHF, CAD, USD, JPY, BRL, etc.			
Examples - Group / OCC	GC = EUR		OCC = EUR	GC = EUR
Additional Remarks	Document Currency - e.g. JPY or GBP entered at the time of document entry	Object Currency (inherited from Co Code to which the cost object belongs to) e.g. Internal Order for GCI1 (USD) will be in USD, Cost Center for GCI2 (CAD) will be in CAD	CCC can be de-activated for Co Codes that have the same currency as that of Controlling Area (e.g. EUR in our example)	
	Document Currency is at times also referred to as Transaction Currency	Reporting Currency - Currency selected in CO Reports (defaulted to Controlling Area Currency)		

Figure 3.12: Currencies in FI and CO

Currencies in FI: GCI assigned both company codes GCI1 (*company code currency* USD—US Dollars) and GCI2 (Currency CAD—Canadian Dollars) to controlling area GCI1 (Currency EUR—Euro). Additionally, GCI set up additional local currencies for company code in configuration transaction OB22. This effectively means that company code GCI1 records transactions in both currencies (USD and EUR). Company code GCI2 records transactions in two currencies—CAD and EUR.

Similarly, if GCI acquired another company in Mexico, Brazil, or Switzerland, those respective company codes would have their own currencies for local legal reporting.

Currencies in CO: Internal reporting would occur in *controlling area currency* EUR since each of these new company codes would be assigned to controlling area GCI1. If GCI had headquarters in Europe or Asia, then it is likely that GCI1 controlling area would have CHF—Swiss Francs or GBP—UK Pounds or JPY—Japanese Yen or CNY—Chinese Yuan as its controlling area currency.

Currencies in CO-PA: Our *operating concern currency* is EUR (same as controlling area currency), and CO-PA reports everything in the operating concern currency of EUR. Additionally, CO-PA captures foreign currency (the same as transaction currency) and company code currency. Note that company code currency can be de-activated for Co Codes that have the same currency as that of the controlling area (e.g., EUR in our example). Such deactivation of company code currency removes data redundancy and frees up a large amount of space in CO-PA tables.

Currencies in Material Ledger: *Material Ledger currency* setup is defined in Material Ledger configuration of "Define Material Ledger Type" in transaction OMX2. In most cases, it is set up as "Currency Transfer from FI." This way, ML inherits currencies from FI.

Transaction currency: GCI is not limited to recording only company code currency (CAD/USD) and controlling area currency (EUR). Financial accounting captures *transaction currency* (for example, SGD—Singapore Dollars) at the financial accounting document level (also known as document currency). This transaction in SGD is translated at the prevailing exchange rate into company code currency (also known as first local currency).

Controlling area currency is also recorded as second local currency (also known as group currency). Thus, financial accounting records three currencies: transaction/document currency, company code/local currency, and controlling area/group currency.

"Thanks for the explanation; this makes it clear." Frank said. "This table provides a good explanation of how currencies are mapped."

3.5   Leverage validation and substitution

"Remember last month when we had an issue with the unintentional transport of sets while transporting validations? Can you tell us if there are any problems that we should be aware of when it comes to validation and substitutions?" Alex emailed Erin.

"Yes, let me know if the information below," Erin responded.

Validation rules involve a validation definition, validation step, prerequisites, validation check, and message.

Validation structure hierarchy is shown in Figure 3.13. This structure is visible in transaction GGB0—validation maintenance. GGB0 is a generic validation transaction across several applications. This includes FI validation (OB28) and CO validation (OKC7) shown elsewhere in this book.

▶ Transaction OB28—Financial Accounting validation

The SAP menu path for validation setup in Financial Accounting is: TOOLS • CUSTOMIZING • IMG • SPRO EXECUTE PROJECT • FINANCIAL ACCOUNTING (NEW) • FINANCIAL ACCOUNTING GLOBAL SETTINGS (NEW) • TOOLS • VALIDATION/SUBSTITUTION • OB28—VALIDATION IN ACCOUNTING DOCUMENTS

▶ Transaction OKC7—Controlling validation

The menu path is as follows: TOOLS • CUSTOMIZING • IMG • SPRO EXECUTE PROJECT • CONTROLLING • GENERAL CONTROLLING • ACCOUNT ASSIGNMENT LOGIC • OKC7—DEFINE VALIDATION

Validation hierarchy has the following structure:

▶ Application Area (e.g. Financial Accounting, Cost Accounting, Profit Center Accounting, Project System)
  ▶ Call-up Point (e.g. Document Header, Line Item)
    ▶ Validation Definition—Table GB93
      ▶ Validation Step—Table GB931
        ▶ Prerequisite (condition) to Validation— Table GB901

Validation structure hierarchy is shown in Figure 3.13.

Other components of Validation:

Rules—Table GB90

Sets—Table GB903

Sets should not be transported!

Sets are generally maintained in each system—they should not be transported. Accidental transport from the development system to the production system would mean overwriting the set data in production. This may lead to data loss and create inconsistencies.

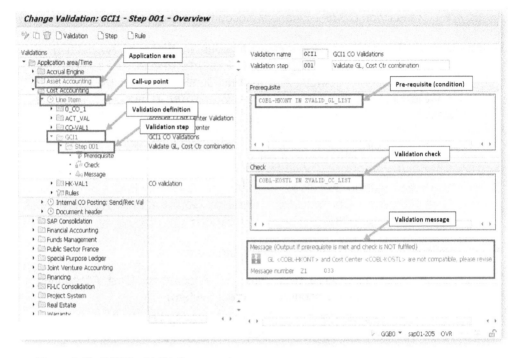

Figure 3.13: GGB0—Validation overview

A few warnings about validations:

► Unlike other areas of SAP configuration, configuration of validation and transport of validation are two separate steps.

► Configuration is carried out at step level, whereas transport is carried out at the validation definition level. This implies that, even if a change is made for a single step, all the steps for the given definition will be included in the transport.

► A validation rule may be modified temporarily and saved in the configuration (or Gold) client. While moving other intended changes for another step, there may be instances where these temporary changes are moved unintentionally to the production system. Therefore, there is a need to define checks at the configuration level to allow for rigorous review and validation before migration.

Substitution follows a similar hierarchy and can be defined in generic transaction GGB1, or the individual module-specific transactions FI substitution (OBBH) and CO substitution (OKC9).

- Application Area (e.g., Financial Accounting, Cost Accounting, Profit Center Accounting, Project System)
  - Call-up Point (e.g., Document Header, Line Item, Complete Document, Order, Cost of Sales Accounting)
    - Substitution Definition—Table GB92
      - Substitution Step—Table GB921
        - Prerequisite (condition) to Substitution—Table GB901
          - Substitution Operation—Table GB922

- Transaction OBBH—Financial Accounting substitution

The SAP menu path for validation setup in Financial Accounting is: TOOLS • CUSTOMIZING • IMG • SPRO EXECUTE PROJECT • FINANCIAL ACCOUNTING (NEW) • FINANCIAL ACCOUNTING GLOBAL SETTINGS (NEW) • TOOLS • VALIDATION/SUBSTITUTION • OBBH—SUBSTITUTION IN ACCOUNTING DOCUMENTS

- Transaction OKC9—Controlling substitution

The menu path is as follows: TOOLS • CUSTOMIZING • IMG • SPRO EXECUTE PROJECT • CONTROLLING • GENERAL CONTROLLING • ACCOUNT ASSIGNMENT LOGIC • OKC9—DEFINE SUBSTITUTION

Generate Validations and Substitutions

 Validations and Substitutions may need to be generated using program RGUGBR00 for them to be activated and updated in underlying programs.

3.6 Understand account assignment

"My accountants are going crazy!" complained Frank. "They have to enter cost centers on all accounting documents. Can we do something about it?"

"We may be able to simplify the data entry a bit, but may not be able to eliminate the entry of cost center on accounting documents," Alex responded.

"Whatever we can do will help my team. They are overwhelmed with the level of detail they have been asked to provide while entering transactions. No doubt, the richness of data has given us a lot of insights in our reporting, but if we can simplify the data capture, then I would love to do so," Frank said.

"Sure, there is something known as *default account assignment* in controlling. It allows you to default cost centers for certain cost elements based on certain rules. If a cost center is explicitly entered on the accounting document, the system will take the cost center entered. However, if no cost center is entered, then the system will default the cost center from the default mapping table," Alex explained.

"That sounds interesting. Can you tell me more about it, please?" Frank was excited.

"Look at Figure 3.14. It shows transaction OKB9 (default account assignment). It has the rules defined for some of the accounts that we use in GCI."

The menu path is as follows: TOOLS • CUSTOMIZING • IMG • SPRO EXECUTE PROJECT • CONTROLLING • COST CENTER ACCOUNTING • ACTUAL POSTINGS • MANUAL ACTUAL POSTINGS • OKB9—EDIT AUTOMATIC ACCOUNT ASSIGNMENT

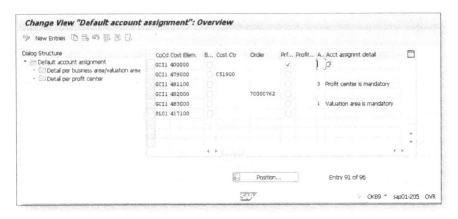

Figure 3.14: OKB9—Default account assignment overview screen

How to interpret OKB9 setup for the given cost elements:

▶ Definition is at the company code and cost element combination.

▶ In terms of default account assignment, we can assign a cost center, an order, profitability segment, or profit center.

▶ There is a way to define account assignment in detail by profit center or valuation area (plant).

▶ 400000 will post to the profitability segment in CO-PA.

▶ 479000 will post to cost center C51900.

▶ 481100 will post based on profit center (see Figure 3.15).

▶ 481100 and profit center 51100 will post to cost center C51102, whereas 481100 and profit center C51900 will post to cost center C51901.

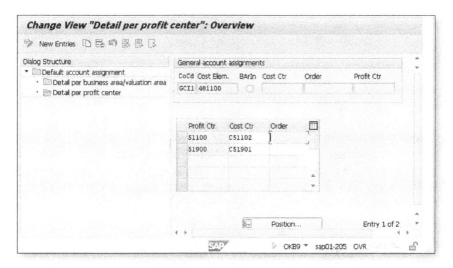

Figure 3.15: OKB9—Detail per profit center

▶ 483000 will post based on valuation area—e.g., plant (see Figure 3.16).

▶ 483000 and plant CHC1 will post to cost center C51101. 483000 and plant CHD1 will post to C51901; 483000 and plant CHD2 will post to C51902.

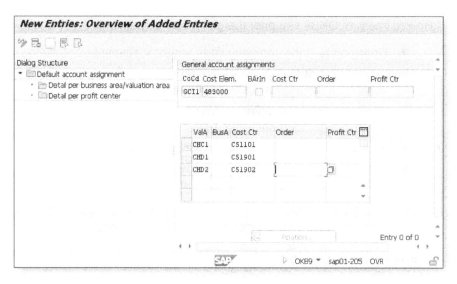

Figure 3.16: OKB9—Detail per valuation area (plant)

"If I have understood this correctly, we can define a direct cost center, or a profit center/plant-based cost center, as default for a given cost element," Frank said.

"Absolutely!" confirmed Alex. "You may not want to set this up for all cost elements. Salaries are one example. You probably want to post salaries to their respective cost centers, rather than a default one. You will need to come up with a list of cost elements and cost center mapping and share them with Erin, and she will get this configured and migrate it across the landscape."

"Makes sense to me. I am thinking I will use this functionality for gain/loss on foreign currency transactions and several other general scrap disposals in the plant. We usually post to the same cost center all the time, so activating this functionality for NCL plants will be helpful in reducing the workload for my team." Frank concluded.

3.7 Synchronize MM-FI fields

"Greg, our Manufacturing Manager at NCL, is reporting an issue that his team is facing at the time of MB1A." Frank said impatiently. "I have not seen this error before; can you help me, Alex?"

"Sure, Frank, I can take a look to see if I can help. Otherwise, we can loop in Erin for her expertise," Alex tried to calm down Frank. "Can you send the details of the error to Erin and me by email?"

Alex and Erin looked at the error message screenshot from the email that Frank forwarded. It was a long email chain starting all the way from the shop floor team to the supervisor, manager, and plant controller. Everyone had tried to weigh in, but nobody seemed to have a clue. The error message read "Fld selectn for mvmt type 261/acct 400000 differs for CO/PP order (011) Message no. M7093". (See Figure 3.17.)

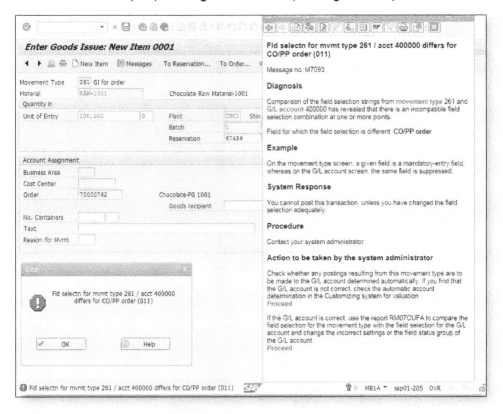

Figure 3.17: MB1A—Good issue to order—error M7-093

"I have never seen this error message at our plant in Chocotown. From the long text of the message, it sounds like this has to do with the field mismatch, but I do not know what would cause it. Can you help us on this, Erin?" Alex asked.

"You are going in the right direction, Alex. This has to do with the field status mismatch between Materials Management (MM) and Financial Accounting (FI)," Erin responded. "This is the first week of go-live at NCL, and this is the first time any consumption is being posted on process orders. Let's look at the program RM07CUFA that is referenced in the error long text," Erin continued.

Erin logged into a test system and went to transaction SE38 (ABAP Editor); the menu path is as follows: TOOLS • ABAP WORKBENCH • DEVELOPMENT • SE38—ABAP EDITOR

Execute program RM07CUFA, enter MOVEMENT TYPE, COMPANY CODE and G/L ACCOUNT found in the error long text (See Figure 3.18).

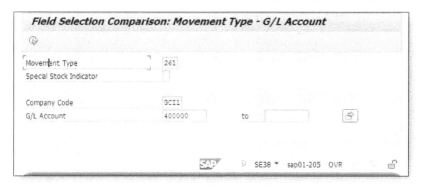

Figure 3.18: SE38—RM07CUFA selection—field selection comparison: movement type—G/L Account

Execute the program for the given selection, and the output (see Figure 3.19) shows information in columns for the field name, the status of the field in movement type, and the status in GL Account.

▶ "+"indicates a required field
▶ "o" indicates an optional field
▶ "-" indicates a suppressed field

If MM has a certain requirement, but FI has the corresponding field as optional, then there is not a field mismatch. However, if MM has a field as required but FI has this field suppressed, then an error would occur due to a mismatch. FI must change this field to either optional or required for this transaction to go through.

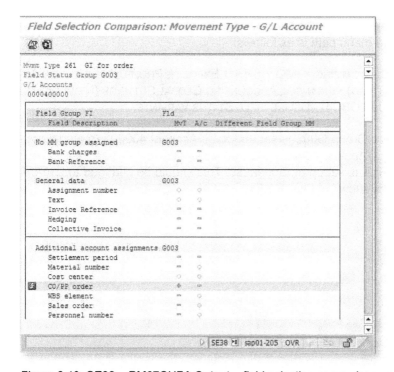

Figure 3.19: SE38—RM07CUFA Output—field selection comparison: movement type—G/L Account

The detailed error log icon ▦ provides additional information on what is causing this field status mismatch (see Figure 3.20).

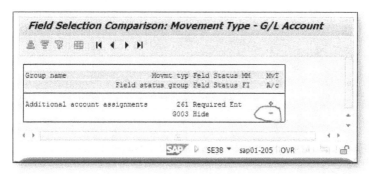

Figure 3.20: SE38—RM07CUFA output—error log

Field for CO/PP Order is a required entry in MM, but this field is hidden in FI, hence the mismatch. A click on hidden field hyperlinks shows the field status group change for GL Account.

There is an alternate transaction for field status groups in GL Accounts: OBC4. The menu path is as follows:

TOOLS • CUSTOMIZING • IMG • SPRO EXECUTE PROJECT • FINANCIAL AC-COUNTING (NEW) • FINANCIAL ACCOUNTING GLOBAL SETTINGS (NEW) • LEDG-ERS • FIELDS • OBC4—DEFINE FIELD STATUS VARIANTS

Field Status Group G003 is set up for GL Account 400000 (material consumption). The ADDITIONAL ACCOUNT ASSIGNMENTS tab has field CO/PP ORDER, which is set up as SUPPRESS. This should be changed to OPTIONAL ENTRY as shown in Figure 3.21.

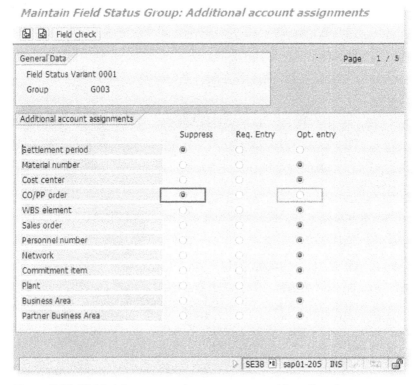

Figure 3.21: Field status group: change suppressed to optional

4 Master data maintenance tips

This chapter provides tips to maintain SAP Controlling master data effectively.

Master data inherits organizational structure information and passes it along to the transaction processing layer. Therefore, it is important to define organization structure, as well as master data attributes, during the design phase and build on the design on an ongoing basis.

Once defined, it is not necessary to make frequent changes in the organization structure. However, the master data needs to be maintained on an ongoing basis. Additionally, master data maintenance is handled by the business—typically, in the production environment.

4.1 Adjust controling master data

Alex received a call from Frank one morning. "I am trying to update several cost centers with costing sheet information, but I can't seem to find a way to do this on a mass basis," Frank said.

"What transaction code are you trying to use?" Alex asked.

"Well, I was given KS02 for cost center change, but this transaction updates information individually. I was also told one KS12 to perform mass changes on cost centers, but this transaction does not seem to have the costing sheet field in the list variant," Frank explained.

"You are headed in the right direction," Alex replied. "KS12 is the correct transaction for cost center mass changes. However, there may be a situation where a specific field is not available for you to update—costing sheet being the case in point," Alex added.

"We will try to set up a new list variant (also known as screen variant). *List variant* in cost center accounting allows collective maintenance of cost centers. There are a number of list variants already available. However, knowing that the field you are looking for is not available, we will set up a new list variant. This is a configuration transaction that Erin showed me some time ago."

List variants are maintained using transaction 0KM1. The SAP menu path is as follows:

TOOLS • CUSTOMIZING • IMG • SPRO EXECUTE PROJECT • CONTROLLING • COST CENTER ACCOUNTING • MASTER DATA • COST CENTERS • 0KM1— DEFINE LIST VARIANTS FOR GROUP PROCESSING

A new list variant ZGCI1 (Costing Sheet on Cost Centers) was set up. As seen in Figure 4.1, the selection and cost center fields are key fields. Costing sheet has been added as a new field in this list variant.

Figure 4.1: 0KM1—Screen Variant ZGCI1 for cost center mass change

Once this list variant is migrated and available in the production environment, these list variants will be available for selection in transaction KS12.

ACCOUNTING • CONTROLLING • COST CENTER ACCOUNTING • MASTER DATA • COST CENTER • COLLECTIVE PROCESSING • KS12—CHANGE

Figure 4.2 shows the KS12 initial screen. ZGCI1 was entered in the LIST VARIANT field.

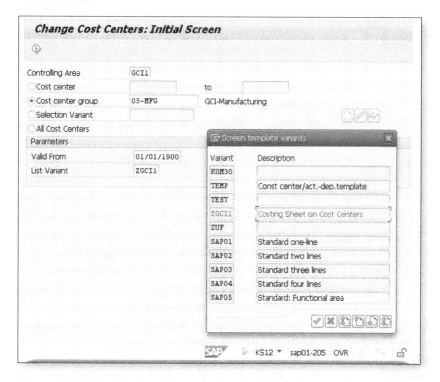

Figure 4.2: KS12—Cost center mass change initial screen

Once the relevant information is entered in the KS12 initial screen, clicking on execute button ⊕ will lead to the output screen.

Costing sheet information can be entered on the respective cost centers as shown in Figure 4.3. Clicking on the save button will save the cost center master data.

107

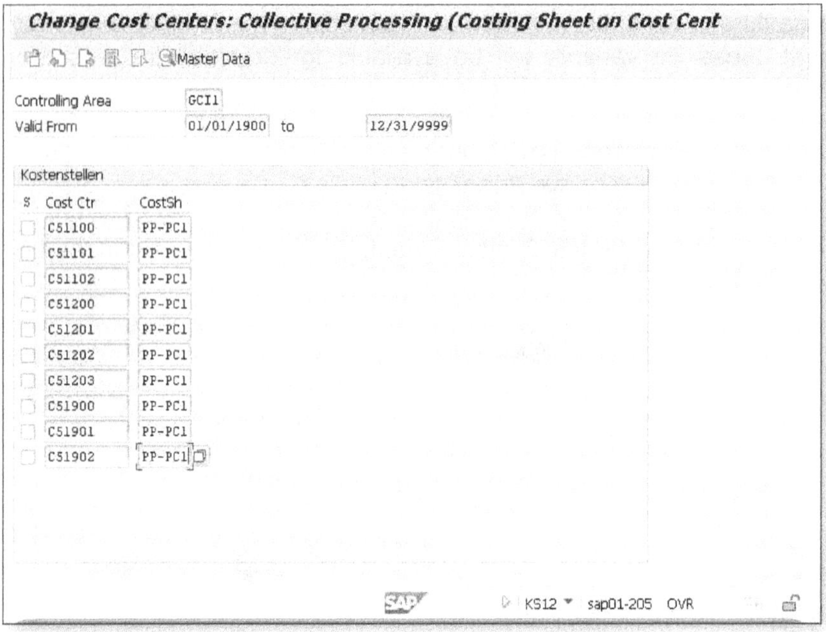

Figure 4.3: KS12—Cost center mass change: output screen

"Bravo, Alex!" exclaimed Frank. "This made my job so much easier. Thanks for showing me this option."

4.2   Change profit center on material

Alex walked into Erin's office. "We have a problem. Remember those new materials that were set up last month for our newly introduced product line? They had an incorrect profit center attached to them. Now, when I asked the master data team to correct the profit centers, they are seeing a bunch of errors while changing them."

"Are you referring to the messages MM-326, MM-327, and MM-335?" Erin asked.

"How did you know about this?" Alex was intrigued.

"I have seen this issue before," Erin explained.

The system may issue the following messages while changing the profit center on Material Master:

▶ MM-326 "There are still open purchase order items or scheduling agreements" (default setup is in error, can be converted to warning)

▶ MM-327 "There are still production orders for the material" (default setup is in error, can be converted to warning)

▶ MM-335 "You want to change the profit center but material stock still exists" (default setup is warning)

Figure 4.4 displays the transaction OMT4 (materials management system messages) where these messages can be changed from error to warning/warning to error.

The SAP Menu path is as follows: TOOLS • CUSTOMIZING • IMG • SPRO EXECUTE PROJECT • LOGISTICS—GENERAL • MATERIAL MASTER • BASIC SETTINGS • OMT4—DEFINE ATTRIBUTES OF SYSTEM MESSAGES

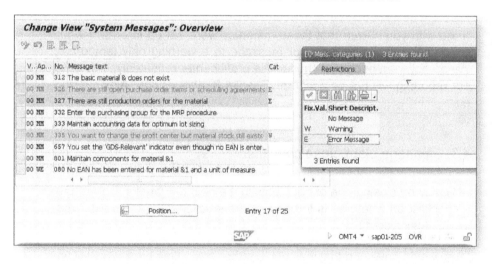

Figure 4.4: OMT4 Message control profit center change

Erin looked up information from SAP's message system to explain why SAP delivers this setup with an error message:

▶ If a GR has already occurred for a material for Profit Center X— Inventory and GRIR postings occurred against the old profit center.

▶ However, when the profit center is changed from X to Y, the invoice will be posted against the new profit center Y, and the GRIR amount will now be against the new profit center.

▶ Additionally, the inventory depletion now takes place against the new profit center, thereby giving a credit balance to the new profit center. The old profit center will continue to have the debit balance for the inventory received.

"It is possible to change these error messages to warning message. Whether we do this on a permanent basis or a temporary basis depends on the business requirement to see inventory transactions at the profit center level," Erin explained.

"Given that MM-335 is set up as a warning message permanently (implying that it may not be important to view inventory balances at profit center level), is there any value in keeping MM-326 and MM-327 as an error? We may need to consider if these two messages should be changed to a warning on a permanent basis, provided you want it that way," Erin continued.

"I am with you. Given that these materials were set up in error, I would recommend changing the error message to a warning only temporarily. We do not want people to change the profit center repeatedly; otherwise, our reporting will not be accurate. Thanks for the insight," Alex concluded.

4.3   Manage plant close checklist

"We may be closing one of our plants in the next few weeks. Do we have a checklist on what needs to occur on transaction data and master data level?" Alex asked Erin.

"Yes, we do have one that was put together some time back. You will find list of steps and the respective transaction codes to accomplish this. You may need to validate if there were any more processes introduced recently. To the best of my knowledge, this list is comprehensive for our setup at GCI. Now, if it is another implementation, then this list will need to be tweaked a bit," Erin responded.

- Close any open purchase orders—ME22N
- Close any open process orders—TECO
- Final WIP, Variance, Settlement—KKAO, KKS1, CO88
- Zero out inventory—MIGO
- Clear DUV cockpit—CKMDUVMAT
- Carry out final ML close—CKMLCP
- Clear cost centers—S_ALR_87013611/FB50
- Lock cost centers—KS12
- Remove cost centers from groups—KSH2
- Move deactivated cost centers in hierarchy—OKEON
- Deactivate allocation cycles—KSV2/KSU2/KEU2
- Change material status to 06—MM02/MM17
- Exclude plant from future ML close runs—CKMLCP
- Transfer profit center balance—FB50
- Lock profit centers—KE52/KE55
- Move deactivated profit centers in hierarchy—KCH5N

4.4   Maintain groups efficiently

"We are replicating the cost center reporting structure from GCI to NCL. Is there a way to do this quickly? There are at least 30 groups with various sub-nodes within them. One, it will be time-consuming, and two, it will be error-prone," Frank's email to Alex read.

"We can use the cost center group download/upload feature," Alex responded.

- Go to transaction KSH3, and identify the appropriate cost center group to be cloned. The menu path is as follows: ACCOUNTING • CONTROLLING • COST CENTER ACCOUNTING • MASTER DATA • COST CENTER GROUP • KSH2—CHANGE
- From the menu, click on EXTRAS • EXPORT as shown in Figure 4.5

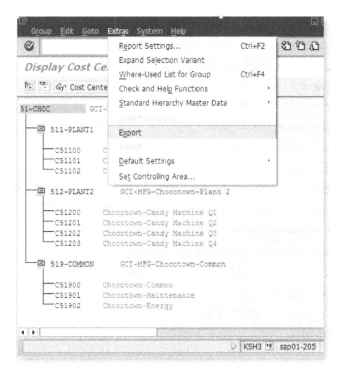

Figure 4.5: KSH3—Export cost center group

▶ A window will open; provide the file path on the local PC

▶ The output will show the set name exported (Figure 4.6)

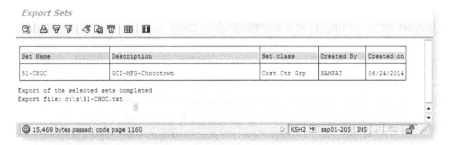

Figure 4.6: KSH3—Export cost center group—result screen

▶ Open the text file; the text file will contain technical details of the set as shown in Figure 4.7

▶ Save this text file with a different name and make necessary changes for the new cost center group

Figure 4.7: KSH3—Export cost center group—text file

▶ Go to transaction KSH2; give the target cost center name

▶ From the menu, click on EXTRAS • IMPORT as shown in Figure 4.8

▶ A window with the file path will open; provide the file path of the new file that was saved on the local PC

▶ The output window will show the set name imported

"Be careful while changing the text file. It can get tricky if the format is changed. Also, make sure you give the target cost center 52-CNDY while importing the set; otherwise, you are likely to overwrite the entire group!" Alex cautioned Frank.

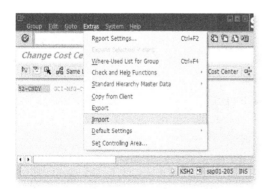

Figure 4.8: KSH2—Import cost center group

113

"Better yet, there is a test system where we had loaded the cost center groups for 52-CNDY; you can review the data, and if everything is fine, then you can export from the test system and import in the production system, Alex concluded

"That sounds like a plan," Frank agreed.

4.5   Utilize material status

The *material status* determines how a material is handled in different applications and in business processes like procurement, MRP, plant maintenance, costing, forecasting, etc. Material status is used to determine which transactions are allowed for the given material status.

"We are implementing material status functionality in all our plants," Erin advised Alex and Frank in an email. "You may want to be aware of which transactions are allowed/disallowed under each material status."

Cross-plant material status maintained in the BASIC DATA view applies to all plants. *Plant-specific material status*es in the plant views (MRP1 and COST 1) override the status in the BASIC DATA view.

Material status and its attributes can be defined in configuration transaction OMS4.

The SAP menu path is as follows: TOOLS • CUSTOMIZING • IMG • SPRO EXECUTE PROJECT • LOGISTICS—GENERAL • MATERIAL MASTER • OMS4—DEFINE MATERIAL STATUSES

An example of possible values in material status is provided below. This is purely an indicative list; a lot would depend upon the organization's needs.

- ▶   10—Material under setup
- ▶   20—Development phase
- ▶   30—Commercial production
- ▶   40—No production, deplete stock
- ▶   50—Obsolete, deletion flag

Flag "A" (warning) would mean a warning message is returned when performing the specific function, whereas a flag "B" (error) would mean an error message is returned when performing the function. Three scenarios are provided below for production order setup:

▶ When material status is 10 ("Material under setup"), a production order should not be allowed to be created. Flag "B" (error) is set for this combination in OMS4. When a user tries to create an order from transaction COR1 or via the MRP run, an error message is returned.

▶ When material status is 20 (Development phase) the production order should be allowed to be created, but with a warning message to the user. Flag "A" (warning) is set for this combination in OMS4. When a user tries to create an order from transaction COR1 or via the MRP run, a warning message is returned.

▶ When material status is 30 (Commercial production), a production order should be allowed to be created, with no messages. Flag "<blank>" (no message) is set for this combination in OMS4.

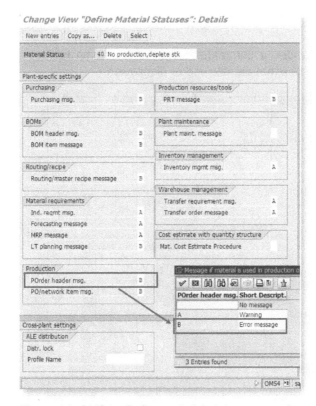

Figure 4.9: OMS4—Define material status—example

115

▶ When material status is 40 (no production, deplete stock), a production order should not be allowed to be created. In Figure 4.9, flag "B" (error) is set for this combination in OMS4. Orders that are already set up are not impacted, but new orders cannot be created.

Figure 4.10 provides a table view of entries maintained for the example material statuses for various business functions.

Data Browser: Table T141: 5 of 5 Hits

MS Description	Pu	BH	BI	RR	IR	RP	PN	PH	PM	IM	Fo	PRT	QMI	TR	TOr	CE	LP
10 Material under setup	A	A	A	A	A	A	B	B	B	B	A	B		B	B		B
20 Development phase	A	A	A	A	A	A	A	B	B	A	B		B	B		B	
30 Commercial production																	
40 No production, deplete stk	B	B	B	B	A	A	B	B		A	A	B		A	A		B
50 Obsolete, deletion flag	B	B	B	B	B	B	B	B		B	B	B		B	B	D	B

SE16 ▾ sap01-205 OVR

Figure 4.10: OMS4—Material status summary (table T141)

Figure 4.11 provides a summarized view with column headers and impacted transactions that are allowed or disallowed.

Material Status	Material Status Description	Purcha sing	BOM head er	BOM item	Routin g / master recipe	Ind. Reqm t	MRP	PO/n etwo rk	PO head er	Plant Main tena nce	Inven tory	Fore casti ng	Produc tion Resour ce Tool msg	QM Inspe ction	Tran sfer requ irem ent	Tran sfer orde r	Mat. Cost Estimat e Procedur e	Long Term Plan ning
10	Material under setup	Warni ng	War ning	War ning	Warni ng	Warn ing	Warni ng	Error	Error	Error	Error	War ning	Error	No mess age	Error	Error	Cost Material	Error
20	Development phase	Warni ng	War ning	War ning	Warni ng	Warn ing	Warni ng	War ning	War ning	Error	Error	War ning	Error	No mess age	Error	Error	Cost Material	Error
30	Commercial production	No messa ge	No mes sage	No mes sage	No messa ge	No mess age	No messa ge	No mes sage	No mes sage	No mes sage	No mess age	No mes sage	No messa ge	No mess age	No mes sage	No mes sage	Cost Material	No mes sage
40	No production, deplete stk	Error	Error	Error	Error	Warn ing	Warni ng	Error	Error	No mes sage	Warn ing	War ning	Error	No mess age	War ning	War ning	Cost Material	Error
50	Obsolete, deletion flag	Error	Error	Error	Error	Error	Error	Error	Error	No mes sage	Error	Error	Error	No mess age	Error	Error	Do Not Cost Material ; Issue Error if Material Compon ent	Error
	Impacted Transaction	ME21N	CS01	CS02	C201	MD11	MD04	COR1	COR1	IW31	MIGO	MP30	CF01	QA01	LB01	LT01	CK11N	MS01

Figure 4.11: Material status allowed/disallowed transactions OMS4 Table T141

4.6   Decode standard costing methods

"Erin, one of the goals given to our department this year is to cost all new products that are introduced—even when they are in the R&D phase. However, when I spoke with our R&D department, they said that they are unable to create a bill of material and recipe for the new materials until the product composition is finalized," Alex said. "This would mean that we will not be able to cost materials that are undergoing research and development. However, since we sell our R&D products sometimes, we need a cost estimate to release the billing document to accounting. Without a cost estimate, our CO-PA valuation strategy returns an error. I only need a rough-cut estimate of the cost, nothing granular or too fancy. However, I do not know how to achieve this without a BOM and a recipe. Do you know if there is any method that can be used for costing?" Alex asked.

"There are multiple ways to perform costing. Let's see if we find anything useful," Erin responded.

"A *cost estimate* is the planned cost of a production cost carrier. It utilizes the BoM and routing (quantity structure) to arrive at the planned cost, which can be transferred to Material Master as a planned price to be utilized in product costing to value the material. The costing variant that controls the cost estimate should be considered for the standard cost estimate. However, there are other ways of setting up a cost estimate and release it to a material master. Let's review these costing methods," Erin continued.

Product costing with quantity structure

As the name suggests, *quantity structure* (e.g., Bill of Material, Routing/Recipe) is used for costing the material. In the absence of the quantity structure, costing procedure gives an error. Product costing with quantity structure is the most commonly used type of standard costing method.

- ▶ Material quantities are derived (read) from the bill of material (BoM or BOM).
- ▶ The components are costed as per the costing method (standard or moving/weighted average), by reading the values stored in the material masters, purchasing information records (PIRs), or some other planned price valuation method like trending (historical average) price.

▶ The activities are costed by applying activity rates as the product moves through the routing (or recipe, in the case of the process industry) or operations performed in the work centers (resources, in the case of process industry) in the manufacturing facility.

▶ Overhead costs are absorbed into the product cost via activity types and/or the costing sheet.

Here is the sequence of costing-related steps:

▶ Cost materials using transaction CK11N

▶ Mark and release materials using CK24

▶ Mass costing, marking, and release are performed using CK40N

The menu path for transaction CK11N is as follows: CONTROLLING • PRODUCT COST CONTROLLING • PRODUCT COST PLANNING • MATERIAL COSTING • COST ESTIMATE WITH QUANTITY STRUCTURE • CK11N—CREATE.

The menu path for transaction CK24 is as follows: CONTROLLING • PRODUCT COST CONTROLLING • PRODUCT COST PLANNING • MATERIAL COSTING • CK24—PRICE UPDATE.

The menu path for transaction CK40N is as follows: CONTROLLING • PRODUCT COST CONTROLLING • PRODUCT COST PLANNING • MATERIAL COSTING • COSTING RUN • EDIT COSTING RUN.

Additive costs

As the name suggests, *additive costs* are over and above the costs set-up, with or without quantity structure. These costs are known ahead of time, based on certain assumptions.

As an example, raw materials are expected to get a certain percentage of freight, duty, and handling costs related overhead. Controllership organization would like to see these costs in their individual buckets, rather than one lump sum amount. Additive costs will help prepare the product cost with individual cost buckets.

Additive costs are set up before the standard costing run is carried out.

The sequence of costing-related steps is:

- ▶ Create additive costs using CK74N (one material at a time)
- ▶ Cost materials using transaction CK11N, and if quantity structure, is used in costing, additive costs are also added to the quantity structure at this time (and hence the term "additive costs")
- ▶ Mark and release materials using CK24
- ▶ Setting up additive costs for multiple materials requires an enhancement
- ▶ Mass costing, marking, and release are done using CK40N, additive costs are added during the costing phase, just like in the case of individual costing

The menu path for transaction CK74N is as follows: CONTROLLING • PRODUCT COST CONTROLLING • PRODUCT COST PLANNING • MATERIAL COSTING • COST ESTIMATE WITH QUANTITY STRUCTURE • ADDITIVE COSTS • CK74N—CREATE.

Product costing without quantity structure

As the name suggests, product costing *without quantity structure* does not use Bill of Material, Routing/Recipe for costing the material. Instead, values are calculated outside the system and input in the screen. Transaction KKPAN is used to set up product costing without quantity structure.

The selection screen for transaction KKPAN resembles CK74N largely because they both point to the same underlying object—*Unit Cost Estimate.* One advantage that KKPAN has over CK74N is that KKPAN can be directly marked and released; there is no need to create a cost estimate as in case of CK74N. Figure 4.12: KKPAN—Cost estimate without quantity structureshows an example of transaction KKPAN

- ▶ Cost materials using transaction KKPAN
- ▶ Mark and release materials using CK24
- ▶ Setting up product costing without a quantity structure for multiple materials requires an enhancement
- ▶ Multiple materials can be marked and released using CK24

The menu path for transaction KKPAN is as follows: CONTROLLING • PRODUCT COST CONTROLLING • PRODUCT COST PLANNING • MATERIAL COSTING • COST ESTIMATE WITHOUT QUANTITY STRUCTURE • KKPAN—CREATE.

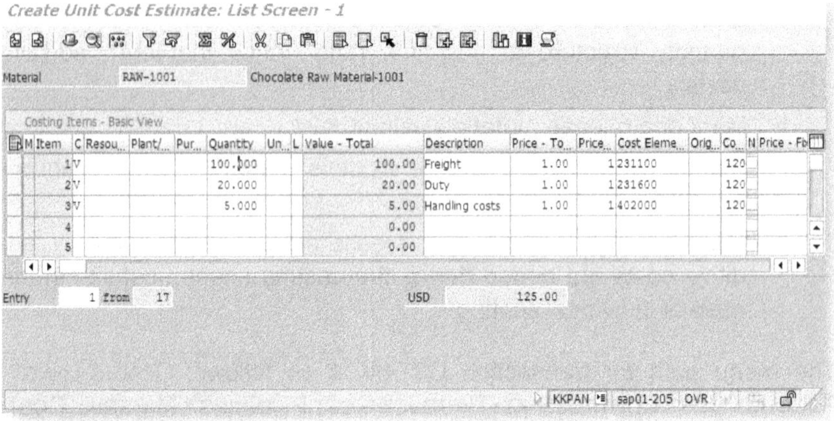

Figure 4.12: KKPAN—Cost estimate without quantity structure

Mixed costing

Mixed costing allows the use of proportions in costing. Mixed costing is used when an organization can procure a component material from multiple sources and/or it can produce a semi-finished/finished material from multiple sources.

The first step is to set up *procurement alternative*. Procurement alternative defines each source of procurement/production; they are set up in transaction CK91N.

The menu path is as follows: CONTROLLING • PRODUCT COST CONTROLLING • PRODUCT COST PLANNING • MATERIAL COSTING • MASTER DATA FOR MIXED COST ESTIMATE • CK91N—EDIT PROCUREMENT ALTERNATIVES

The next step is to define mixing ratios, which define the proportion of purchase/production. These proportions will be used to create a weighted average cost for the purchased/produced material.

The menu path is as follows: CONTROLLING • PRODUCT COST CONTROLLING • PRODUCT COST PLANNING • MATERIAL COSTING • MASTER DATA FOR MIXED COST ESTIMATE • MIXING RATIOS • CK94—CREATE/CHANGE

The sequence of costing related steps is:

- Create procurement alternatives using CK91N (one material at a time)
- Set up mixing ratios using CK94 (one material at a time)
- Cost materials using transaction CK11N, quantity structure from individual cost estimates if any, are used in costing, mixing ratios are used to arrive at the weighted average cost for the material
- Mark and release materials using CK24
- Setting up procurement alternatives and mixing ratios for multiple materials requires an enhancement
- Mass costing, marking, and release are done using CK40N, and procurement alternatives and mixing ratios are used during the costing phase, just like in the case of individual costing

"It sounds like what we need for our R&D materials is product costing without quantity structure, is that correct?" Alex said.

"Exactly, Alex." Erin confirmed. "Since the quantity structure does not exist for such materials, there is no point in using product costing with quantity structure," Erin continued. "What we should do is to ask R&D for some high-level estimates for each type of R&D material, and we can use them while setting up the standard cost estimates. Since the volume of materials is not too high, I recommend we start with manual mainte- nance. If the volume increases, then we can look at developing an en- hancement that can allow us to create multiple cost estimates at the same time," Erin concluded.

"I agree. That sounds like a plan," Alex said. "Thank you so much for your help, Erin!"

4.7 Discover active ingredient functionality

"The quality team is telling me that we have been having issues with milk purchases," Bob rushed into Alex's office and said. "It sounds like milk vendors are supplying milk with lower fat content lately but are charging us the same price as before. We are tracking the fat content by batch, but this is being recorded manually outside the system. There currently is no way of recording fat content by each batch in the system. This is affecting the yield at production. Variances are all over the place," Bob continued.

"It sounds like effectively, we are paying more for milk." Alex was trying make sense out of the situation. "That sounds a bit counter-intuitive. If I were to use a simplified supermarket example, whole milk is the most expensive, 2 percent fat content milk is a few cents less, 1 percent milk is even less expensive, and fat-free milk is the cheapest of them all," Alex said.

"You have come up with a great analogy, Alex. This is exactly the same situation, but it's not one or two gallons that we buy for our homes. We are looking at thousands of gallons of milk that we use for our operations each month. So you can imagine the financial impact," Bob said. "Our Plant Manager, Carl, told me that our situation has something to do with the way we had set up milk procurement. We are not using the standard functionality of active ingredient management, but we think that using this feature may help us address this issue to some extent and pay the vendors based on how much fat is contained in the milk they supply to us, rather than the volume or weight," Bob continued.

"Really? We should definitely look for a systematic way of doing this. I haven't heard of this functionality in SAP, but I can do some research," Alex said. Alex was neither involved in the milk procurement processes nor did he know anything about active ingredient management functionality in SAP. However, he thought he could take this assignment as an opportunity to learn something new.

"That would be great, Alex!" Bob said. "Can you please investigate this with the help of the procurement, quality, and IT teams to see if you can put in a proposal on how we can improve this process?" Bob concluded.

"Sure, Bob, I'll do that."

After several days of research and discussion with Erin and others, Alex came up with a white paper, which he presented to Bob.

Overview of Active Ingredient Management

Active Ingredient Management functionality is used mainly in a process industry where each batch can have a different proportion of the active ingredient. As in case of milk, fat content may differ for each batch/supplied quantity. Since the fat content can have such a big impact on the yield (productivity) as well as the ultimate cost of milk (payment to the vendor is based on fat content), there is a need to measure each batch separately and value each batch according to the fat content.

Composition or attributes of products vary. We cannot use a fixed conversion factor to convert quantities of these products into various units of measure. Instead, each batch has to be given an individual conversion factor. Goods movements and stock movements for these materials are carried out in physical quantities. Valuation, costing, availability checks, and planning, however, are carried out based on the active ingredient quantity.

Other terms used for this functionality are potency calculation, potent materials tracking, potency factor, potent material, batch-specific unit of measure, active ingredient management, batch-specific split valuation, and valuation relevant proportion units.

Features of SAP Active Ingredient Management

- ▶ Each batch of produced or purchased active ingredient material needs to be valued separately.
- ▶ Each active ingredient material is created with Split Valuation (e.g., Batch Level valuation).
- ▶ Standard potency is stored in Material Master; standard valuation is stored in a specific transaction.
- ▶ Each batch is valued based on the actual potency, based on this information.
- ▶ Depending on the timing of the goods receipt and the timing of the recording of the potency result, the system adjusts the value of the material and post the difference to the re-valuation account.
- ▶ There may be a need to reclassify this re-valuation difference into purchase price variance (if purchased) or material usage variance (if produced)
- ▶ The base unit of measure is Logistic Unit. The alternate UOM is Potent Unit.
- ▶ Potent Unit is maintained as a batch characteristic.
- ▶ Batch-Level Split Valuation is active.

- Total Inventory is valued at a moving average, but potent content is valued at Standard (Inventory Value = Quantity for each batch * Actual Potency of each batch * Standard cost of Potency).

Material Master setup

- Material Master—Basic Data view: Base Unit of Measure is set up in Weight/Volume/Physical Unit—e.g., kilograms, grams, or liter

- Material Master Basic Data tab (cross-plant): An alternate unit is set up in the active ingredient unit—grams of active ingredient

- Material Master Additional Data: The proportionate units tab (cross-plant) is maintained with the default potency

- Material Master Additional Data: Unit of Measure Conversion tab—the conversion is maintained between the weight unit and potency unit

- Accounting 1 view: Activation of Batch-Level Split Valuation (Valuation Category "X"), Price Control of Moving Average "V" at the header material

- Underlying Batches valued at Price Control of Standard Price "S" (Valuation Type as each individual batch

- Standard cost is maintained for the proportionate unit (potency) in Transaction Code MWB1

- Sales View 1: Sales Unit = AI Unit (KGA/GA)

- Sales View 1: Sales Unit not Var = Always checked—cannot change Sales Unit in Sales Order

- Purchasing View: Order Unit = AI Unit (KGA/GA)

- Purchasing View: Var. OUn = <blank> "Not Active"—cannot change Order Unit in Purchase Order

- Accounting 1 View: Valuation Category = "X" i.e. Split Valuation must be active (very important, need to set up new material if this is missed out)

- Accounting 1 View: Price Control for header material = "V"

- Accounting 1 View: Price Control for individual batches (Batch = Valuation type) = "S"

Other cautions:

► Purchase price in PIR is expressed in AI Unit (KGA/GA), POs get created in AI Order Unit

► Sales price is expressed in AI Unit (KGA/GA); sales orders get created in AI Sales Unit

► Transaction MWB1: Price exists in AI Unit

► Material must be costed, and standard price must be released before any transaction is carried out

► Cutover: Batch characteristic and potency must be maintained before the 561 inventory load is carried out. Otherwise, the system uses the default potency, thereby creating a mismatch in inventory values between two systems

► Periodic batch job is used to call MWBQ for systemic PO history update so that invoices are paid based on actual potency

► Month-end reclassification may be necessary from revaluation to purchase prices variance/manufacturing usage variance

► A characteristic entry should be made prior to recording a usage decision

Process overview

► Materials are set up with valuation-relevant proportion units, with split valuation, and with the standard cost for proportion valuation maintained in MWB1.

► A purchase order is created in KGAs, goods receipt is done in KGs, and goods are received at standard potency proportion.

► Quality results are recorded for the inspection lot using T Code QA32. Actual potency percentage derived from testing is recorded. If the actual potency is higher than the standard potency, the system automatically posts an entry (reverse impact if the actual potency is lower than the standard potency).
  ► Debit Inventory (BSX)
  ► Credit Revaluation (UMB)

► Update purchase order history with the actual potency using T Code MWBQ, and the following entry gets posted:
  ► Credit GRIR (WRX)
  ► Debit Price Variance (PRD)

- ▶ Enter the invoice using transaction MIRO, and the total value of the postings made into GRIR for this purchase order is pulled in by SAP. This is standard cost per KGA X actual KGA received.
- ▶ At period end, post the following manual journal entry to nullify the postings made to revaluation and price variance:
  - ▶ Debit Revaluation
  - ▶ Credit Price Variance

The above process keeps the accounts and postings relatively neat and tidy (including taking care of the Accounts Payable aspect) and at the same time provides the business with the benefits of the active ingredients functionality.

"This is a great document, Alex!" Bob exclaimed. "I understand there is a lot of benefit to using this functionality. I am going to circulate this note to others in the organization and see if they would like to implement this design. Thanks for putting this together."

5 Leverage reporting and reconciliation

This section provides tips to leverage SAP Controlling for data reporting and reconciliation.

Financial Accounting (FI) is all about data capture and external reporting, whereas Controlling (CO) is all about internal reporting. FI and CO largely complement each other. SAP software is an integrated system, and all financial transactions are captured in Financial Accounting. Controlling supports internal reporting requirements.

5.1 Analyze MM-FI accounting flow

Transaction OBYC MM-FI account determination forms the core of SAP's integration between the Materials Management (MM), Financial Accounting (FI), and Controlling (CO) modules.

"I have been trying to reconcile postings coming into FI from Materials Management and don't know where to start," Frank wrote in an email to Alex. "Will you be able to help me with this?"

"Definitely," Alex said. "Let's talk to Erin; she knows a lot about MM and FI."

Figure 5.1 provides a summary of movement types and accounting entries. Business process is listed in the column furthest to the left, with movement type in the next column, and the debit and credit posting in the subsequent columns. There is a column for transaction and account modifiers; these are SAP's terms for logically grouping similar types of transactions. The transaction account modifier, along with the valuation class, drives the accounting entries.

Transaction keys are used to determine general ledger accounts used by the system. Account modifier is used to differentiate account determinations, depending on the procedure.

Transaction keys are predefined in the SAP system and cannot be changed. The transaction account modifier and the valuation class drive the accounting entries.

Process	Movement Type - Description	Transaction-Account Modifier	Debit GL	Debit GL Description	Transaction-Account Modifier	Credit GL	Credit GL Description
Purchase of Raw Material	101 - Goods receipt for Purchase Order	BSX	300000	Inventory - Raw Material	WRX	191100	Goods Received / Invoice Received
Consumption of Raw Materials to Process Order	261 - Goods Issue for order	GBB-VBR	400010	Raw materials consumed	BSX	300000	Inventory - Raw Material
Production of Semi-Finished Materials for Process Order	101 - Goods receipt for Process Order	BSX	790000	Unfinished products	GBB-AUF	895000	Factory output of production orders
Consumption of Semi-Finished Materials to Process Order	261 - Goods Issue for order	GBB-VBR	890000	Semi-finished products consumed	BSX	790000	Unfinished products
Production of Finished Materials for Process Order	101 - Goods receipt for Process Order	BSX	792000	Finished goods inventory	GBB-AUF	895000	Factory output of production orders
Sampling for Quality Inspection	331 - Goods Issue to sampling Quality Inspection	GBB-VQP	237000	Losses - consumption of quality control	BSX	792000	Finished goods inventory
Sale of Finished Material	601 - Goods issue: delivery	GBB-VAX	892000	Change in finished products inventory	BSX	792000	Finished goods inventory
Scrapping of Finished Material	551 - Goods Issue for scrapping	GBB-VNG	890001	Scrapped material - own production	BSX	792000	Finished goods inventory
Cycle Count (Physical Inventory) of Finished Material	701 - Goods receipt for physical inventory adjustment	BSX	792000	Finished goods inventory	GBB-INV	233000	Losses - inventory variance
Initial Inventory Load of Finished Material	561 - Initial entry of stock balances	BSX	792000	Finished goods inventory	GBB-BSA	799999	Inventory migration
Consumption of Raw Material from Sub-Contractor stock (special stock "O")	543 - Goods Issue from stock at sub-contractor	GBB-VBO	400010	Raw materials consumed	BSX	300000	Inventory - Raw Material
Production of Finished Goods by Sub-Contractor (Production)	101 - Goods receipt from sub-contractor	BSX	792000	Finished goods inventory	BSV	893010	Sub-contract stock change
Production of Finished Goods by Sub-Contractor (Tolling Fee)	101 - Goods receipt from sub-contractor	FRL	417001	Purchased services	WRX	191100	Goods Rcvd/Invoice Rcvd

Figure 5.1: Movement types and accounting entries

The transaction key in MM-FI account determination is not the same as transaction code. A transaction code is an alphanumeric code that represents a particular task in SAP. It allows users to access tasks directly without having to use menu paths.

"You may have seen an accounting entry at the time of the purchase of raw material as a debit to inventory and credit GR/IR," Erin said. "Well, the configuration setup of transaction BSX (inventory posting) is responsible for the inventory posting, and WRX (GR/IR clearing account) is responsible for GR/IR posting. Therefore, when movement type 101 is used to record the goods receipt of raw material (valuation class 3000) for a purchase order, the system looks up the GL Account for transaction BSX and WRX for valuation class 3000 and records it in the accounting document.

"Similarly, when this raw material is consumed using movement type 261, the system looks up transaction GBB (offsetting entry for inventory posting) for account modifier VBR (consumption for internal goods issues), and that reflects the GL Account in the accounting document.

"The OBYC MM-FI account determination configuration is set up at the time of original implementation, and once set up, these accounts are derived behind the scenes. You'll want to test the setup before going live to ensure that the correct accounts are being hit for the respective transactions. You can change this configuration after go-live, but the revised setup needs to be thoroughly tested. Otherwise, we may run the risk of impacting regular operations." Erin concluded.

"Thank you, Erin. I understand now," Alex said. "The other day I had an audit query where the auditors wanted me to provide GL postings for all samples consumed for quality inspection for one of our finished materials. I looked things up and saw that every material document that had movement type 331 had the same accounting impact. Now I know that the system was using GBB-VQP and BSX for the posting."

5.2   Interpret valuation of goods movement

"How come the reversal document of consumption has different values than the original document?" Greg asked Frank. Greg is the Manufacturing Manager at NCL, the company that was acquired by GCI. NCL's SAP implementation was a few months old and had been stabilized. However, some reporting and data flow-related questions were popping up every so often.

"It should be the same, except for rounding differences," Frank said.

"Yes, these are rounding differences, but I wonder what causes them." Greg was still confused.

"Let me ask Alex and Erin if they know, and I will get back to you," Frank responded.

Alex and Erin pointed to an SAP note on this topic, SAP note "212286—Overview note—Valuation during goods movements":

For materials controlled by a standard price, receipts are posted in proportion to the price, but issues are posted in proportion to the value.

- ▶ Value determination with proportion to price (e.g., for goods receipts):
    - ▶ Value of stock posting = (Standard price * quantity)/price unit

  ▶ Value determination with proportion to value (e.g., for goods issue):

  ▶ Value of stock posting = (Total value of stock * quantity)/entire valuated stock

In other words, good receipts will match to the standard price, but goods issues will use a price in proportion to value.

This information was shared with Greg, and he was now convinced on why consumption posting and its reversal had some rounding differences.

5.3   Separate GR/IR for intercompany

"Corporate wants to separate GR/IR into third-party and intercompany," Bob's email to Alex read. "Since we have had a lot of internal goods transfers within the group, it is becoming increasingly difficult to identify which transactions belong to intercompany and which belong to third party vendors. GR/IR ageing has been a point of focus lately. The purchasing team is unable to help us in ageing analysis since there is no clear-cut demarcation. Can you work with Erin to find out if there is a systemic way for us to achieve this?"

Alex thought that this looked like a very genuine requirement. He was not sure why this hadn't been thought of yet. Maybe because it is only recently GCI has had many internal transactions as Bob had highlighted.

Erin looked up the system and found a way to achieve this systematically. Alex took notes to present to Bob and others in the company.

Background and need:

  ▶ Our current design has third party GR/IRs as well as intercompany GR/IRs all posting to the same account—191100 Goods Rcvd/Invoice Rcvd (third party)—see Figure 5.2.

  ▶ Even intercompany stock transport orders point to the same GL Account 191100, thereby making it difficult to separate the two.

- ▶ A month-end adjustment entry is manually made between 191100 and 191000—Goods Rcvd/Invoice Rcvd (own production).
- ▶ There is a need to separate GR/IR between intercompany and third party transactions in a systematic way.
- ▶ Third party transactions should continue to go to 191100.
- ▶ Intercompany transactions should now be pointed to GL 191000.

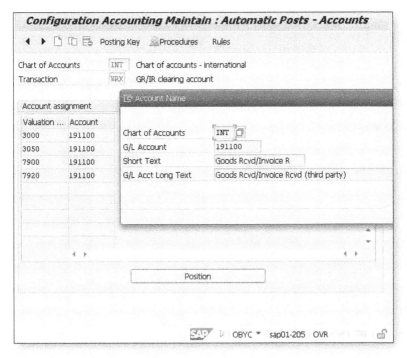

Figure 5.2: OBYC—Current setup of WRX: GR/IR clearing account

Approach to separate third party versus intercompany GR/IR

The SAP menu path for MM-FI account determination configuration is: TOOLS • CUSTOMIZING • IMG • SPRO EXECUTE PROJECT • MATERIALS MANAGEMENT • VALUATION AND ACCOUNT ASSIGNMENT • ACCOUNT DETERMINATION • ACCOUNT DETERMINATION WITHOUT WIZARD • OMWB—CONFIGURE AUTOMATIC POSTINGS • OBYC—ACCOUNT ASSIGNMENT

▶ Activate user exit LMR1M002 (Account grouping for GR/IR account maintenance)

▶ Influence GL Account used for GR/IR via OBYC Account Determination for Transaction WRX (GR/IR clearing account)—see Figure 5.3

    ▶ Account modifier (T030-KOMOK) YRX for third party transactions

    ▶ Account modifier (T030-KOMOK) ZRX for intercompany transactions

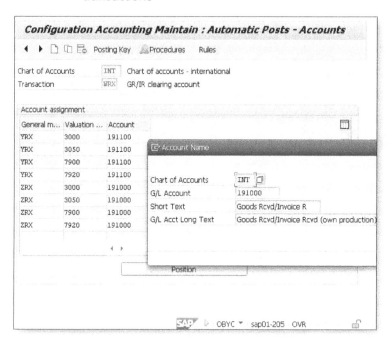

Figure 5.3: OBYC—Proposed setup of WRX: GR/IR clearing account

User exit info and suggested logic:

▶ Activate user exit LMR1M002 (Account grouping for GR/IR account maintenance). See Figure 5.4.

▶ This user exit will be invoked during all Logistics Invoice Verification (LIV) transactions.

The SAP Menu path is: TOOLS • CUSTOMIZING • IMG • SPRO • EXECUTE PROJECT • MATERIALS MANAGEMENT • LOGISTICS INVOICE VERIFICATION • MAINTAIN CUSTOMER EXITS AND BUSINESS ADD-INS • CMOD—MAINTAIN CUSTOMER EXITS FOR INVOICE VERIFICATION

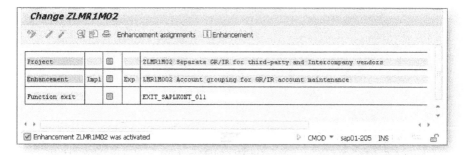

Figure 5.4: CMOD: Logistics Invoice Verification (LIV) user exit activation LMR1M002

▶ User exit LMR1M002 includes function module EXIT_SAPLKONT_011 (Account grouping for GR/IR account determination) See Figure 5.5

▶ This function module has the program ZXM08U18 that will in turn allow for influence of account modifier T030-KOMOK (usually blank).

▶ Vendor account group (field KTOKK) will be used to identify intercompany or third party transactions.

▶ Vendor account group 0007 (plants) is used for intercompany transactions, whereas all other vendor groups are for third-party transactions.

▶ System should post to regular GR/IR or intercompany GR/IR based on the following logic:

　　▶ If LFA1-KTOKK = "0007" (Plants), then use KOMOK-ZRX [191000—Goods Rcvd/Invoice Rcvd (own production)]

　　▶ If LFA1-KTOKK <> "0007" (Plants), then use KOMOK-YRX [191100 -Goods Rcvd/Invoice Rcvd (third party)]

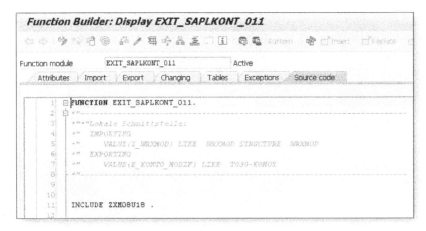

Figure 5.5: CMOD: Logistics Invoice Verification (LIV) program ZXM08U18

Treatment of open GR/IR transactions

If it is determined that the user exit program sends old transactions to old account and only new intercompany transactions to the new setup, then this logic should also be built into the same program.

5.4 Simplify inventory reconciliation

"Hey, Erin, do you remember when Dave was with us last year and all three of us looked at the MM-FI inventory reconciliation issue?" Alex asked Erin.

"Oh yes, I remember that day. We looked at various transactions like MMBE, MB52, and MB51 on the materials management side and MB5L on the stock values side," Erin responded.

"Exactly! Well, I came across a report that may do something similar to MB5L!" Alex said. He was pleased that he had found this new transaction code.

"Really? Let's look." Now Erin was curious.

The new transaction code that Alex had found was FAGL_MM_RECON. The SAP menu path is as follows: ACCOUNTING • FINANCIAL ACCOUNTING • GENERAL LEDGER • PERIODIC PROCESSING • CLOSING • CHECK/COUNT •

FAGL_MM_RECON—BALANCE COMPARISON: GENERAL LEDGER—MATERIALS MANAGEMENT

Figure 5.6 has the snapshot of the initial screen of FAGL_MM_RECON.

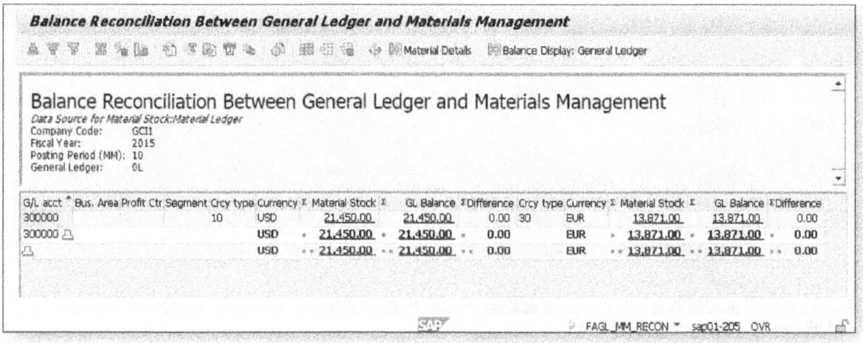

Figure 5.6: FAGL_MM_RECON—Balance reconciliation between GL and MM—summary screen

Figure 5.7 has the snapshot of FAGL_MM_RECON detail screen, which provides information by material.

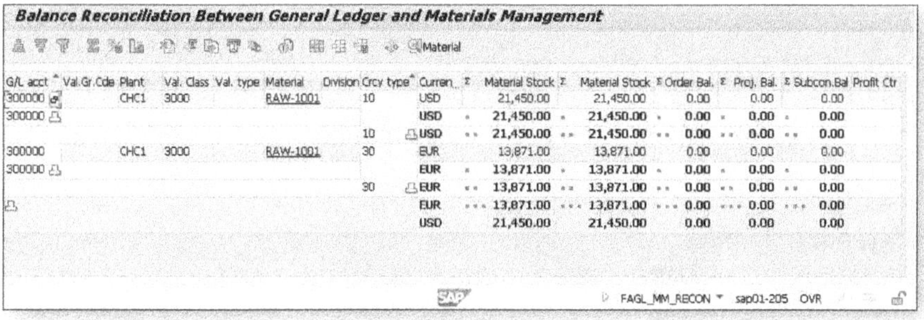

Figure 5.7: FAGL_MM_RECON—Balance reconciliation between GL and MM—material detail screen

"This looks promising!" Erin exclaimed. "Can we compare how MB5L and MB52 look? This is the real-time inventory. However, both MB5L and FAGL_MM_RECON seem to have year/period in the selection screen, so technically speaking, we can run them for immediate inventory on hand, as well as for the inventory at prior month-end."

Alex went to transaction MB5L (see Figure 5.8) using the menu path:

LOGISTICS • MATERIALS MANAGEMENT • INVENTORY MANAGEMENT • PERIODIC PROCESSING • MB5L—LIST OF STOCK VALUES.

The inventory balance was same in both reports FAGL_MM_RECON and MB5L. MB5L did not allow drill-down at material, GL balance level, but FAGL_MM_RECON had a drill-down feature to material balances as well GL balances.

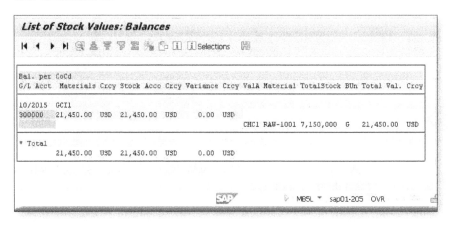

Figure 5.8: MB5L—List of stock values

"Now, let's look at MB52 and see if these numbers tie too," Erin said.

Alex went to MB52 (see Figure 5.9) using the menu path: LOGISTICS • MATERIALS MANAGEMENT • INVENTORY MANAGEMENT • ENVIRONMENT • STOCK • MB52—WAREHOUSE STOCK.

Display Warehouse Stocks of Material

Material	Plnt	SLoc	SL	Batch	BUn	Unrestricted	Crcy	Value Unrestricted
RAW-1001	CHC1	0001		1	G	7,150,000	USD	21,450.00
*							USD	21,450.00

☑ Layout was applied   MB52 ▼ sap01-205 OVR

Figure 5.9: MB52—Warehouse Stock

"This is a very good find, Alex!" Erin congratulated Alex on finding this new transaction code, which they had never used before. "I am certain this will be useful for the accountants for month-end reconciliation."

5.5 Navigate from Report to Transaction

Alex was looking at one of the reports that Erin had developed for GCI. However, he was not able to drill down from the report to the actual posting. This seemed to be a problem, given that most of the standard reports have this feature. Alex decided to call Erin and ask her if there was a way to do so.

First, we go to transaction GR52, which is report group change. The menu path is as follows: ACCOUNTING • CONTROLLING • COST CENTER ACCOUNTING • INFORMATION SYSTEM • TOOLS • REPORT PAINTER • REPORT GROUP • GR52—CHANGE

As shown in Figure 5.10, click on CONFIGURE, this will open up a pop-up window. There is an icon for ADD, WHICH should look like this. Another window will open up; click on [Other Report Type] .

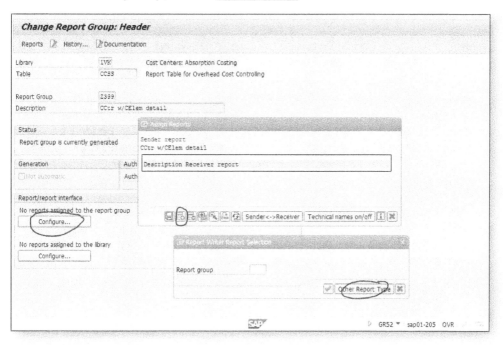

Figure 5.10: GR52—Report Group change header

Select TR (Transaction) in the next window as shown in Figure 5.11. This allows you to add the desired transaction to the report.

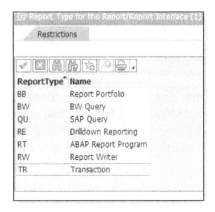

Figure 5.11: GR52—Add Transaction to Report Group

Figure 5.12: GR52—Add Transaction KSB1-Cost Center Line Items

As shown in Figure 5.12, Erin added transaction KSB1, which is nothing but Cost Centers: Actual Line Items display. Additionally, Erin added another report, COST CENTERS: BREAKDOWN BY PARTNER, transaction KS03 for DISPLAY COST CENTER and transaction KA03 for DISPLAY COST ELEMENT

The drill-down would now show these four options as shown in Figure 5.13.

"You should be all set now!" Erin said. "Do you want to try running the report again to see if you are able drill down to the line items?"

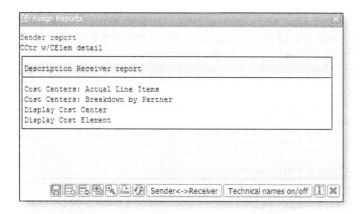

Figure 5.13: GR52 –Report Group now has three transactions

"Sure. I am eager to see how this will look," Alex responded. Alex went to transaction GR55 to run the report again. The menu path is as follows: ACCOUNTING • CONTROLLING • COST CENTER ACCOUNTING • INFORMATION SYSTEM • TOOLS • REPORT PAINTER • REPORT GROUP • GR55—EXECUTE.

Once the report output showed up on the screen, Alex double-clicked on one of the rows. Indeed, he saw these four options available for drill-down (see Figure 5.14).

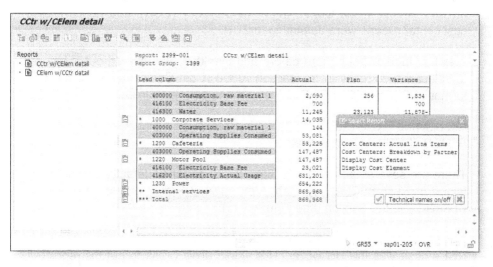

Figure 5.14: GR55—Execute Report—Drill Down shows four options

Alex clicked on COST CENTERS: ACTUAL LINE ITEMS to go to transaction KSB1 line item postings. Later, he came back to the same screen and selected DISPLAY COST CENTER to review the description of the cost center in transaction KS03.

"Thanks for making this work. This seemed like so simple, yet so beneficial to end-users like me," Alex said.

5.6   Explore Cost Center Reporting settings

Frank seemed a bit frustrated on the phone. "Each time I run cost center plan versus actual report, it gives me the output in EUR. I need to apply the exchange rate conversion factor from EUR to USD in order for me to get the number in Mexican Pesos. Alex, do you know of an option where I can tell the system to give me the output in USD?"

Alex knew exactly what Frank was experiencing. GCI was using Euro (currency code EUR) as the Controlling area currency, whereas Company Code NCL was set up with US Dollar (currency code USD). Being responsible for the US operations of NCL, it made sense for Frank to look for data in US Dollars. However, Frank's user settings were set to give the output in the Controlling Area Currency (EUR), and hence his cost center reports were defaulting to EUR.

Alex had himself been there before and thankfully had figured out a way to select the currency in transaction RPC0 (Cost Center Accounting Information System: User Settings). The menu path is as follows:

ACCOUNTING • CONTROLLING • COST CENTER ACCOUNTING • INFORMATION SYSTEM • RPC0—USER SETTINGS

There are several tabs in transaction RPC0; currency defaults are maintained in REPORT CURRENCY tab. Alex advised Frank to select OBJECT CURRENCY in this section (see Figure 5.15).

Object currency is inherited from the company code currency, which in NCL's case was the US Dollar. This would allow Frank to get his report output defaulted in US Dollars.

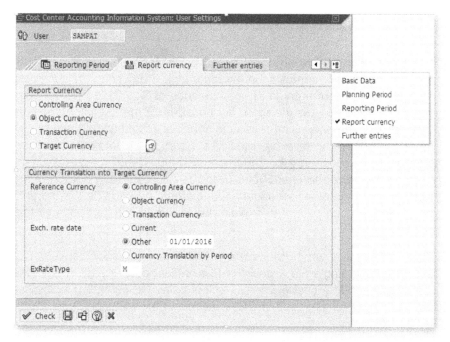

Figure 5.15: RPC0—Cost Center Information System: User Settings

"This is very useful!" exclaimed Frank. "Thanks for showing me this feature. Will all my reports now default to object currency?" Frank wanted to confirm.

"RPC0 applies to Cost Center reports only. There are similar transactions for other sub-modules of Controlling." Alex responded.

▶ RPA0—Cost and Revenue Element Accounting Information System: User Settings

▶ RPB0: Activity-Based Costing Information System: User Settings

▶ RPC0—Cost Center Accounting Information System: User Settings

▶ RPO0—Internal Orders Information Systems: User Settings

▶ RPP0—Project Systems Information System: User Settings

"Thank you Alex. I will be sure to change my user settings in each of the areas," Frank concluded.

5.7   Leverage CO Substitution

"Cost allocations between cost objects using secondary cost elements are creating a lot of confusion in my reporting," Frank said. "All such cost flows send an in/out entry in FI, total balance of GL 499999 (Reconciliation FI-CO) is zero. It is therefore not possible for me to explain the flow between departments using reports in financial accounting. I have to use reports in controlling to explain this. I am particularly interested in postings going to secondary cost element 640000 (Benefits Accrual Overhead) to be posted to GL 450000 (Benefits Accrual). I am not too much worried about the other secondary cost element postings; this is the only one that has been painful to explain. Do you think we can address this specific issue?"

Alex knew exactly what Frank meant. *Real-time integration* between CO and FI uses a single GL Account in FI to reflect cost allocation postings that use secondary cost elements. GCI is using GL 499999 (Reconciliation FI-CO), which is set up in OBYC Account determination under transaction CO1.

"Let's write down the current state and the proposed state, which will help us better visualize and figure out if there is a way to handle this systematically," Alex responded.

Current postings:

▶   CO side:

Debit GL 640000, cost center C51101

Credit GL 640000, cost center C51900

▶   FI side:

Debit GL 499999, cost center C51101

Credit GL 499999, cost center C51900

Proposed postings:

▶   CO side:

Debit GL 640000, cost center C51101

Credit GL 640000, cost center C51900

► FI side:

Debit GL 450000, cost center C51101

Credit GL 450000, cost center C51900

Essentially, we do not need any change on the CO side. Change is requested on the FI side such that if the CO side cost element is 640000, then we want the generic GL 499999 to be replaced with GL 450000.

"Have I stated the requirement accurately?" Alex asked.

"You are right on. This is exactly what we need!" Frank exclaimed. "As I mentioned, I do not have an issue with the remaining secondary cost elements. I am worried only about 640000 postings."

"We will set up CO Substitution so that the system posts to a different GL Account on FI side." Figure 5.16 shows snapshot of transaction OKC9 (CO substitution).

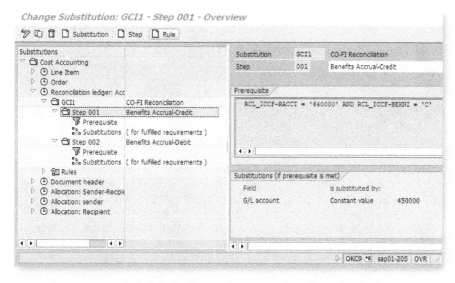

Figure 5.16: OKC9—CO Substitution for GL Account in place of CO-FI Reconciliation Account

The menu path is as follows: TOOLS • CUSTOMIZING • IMG • SPRO EXECUTE PROJECT • CONTROLLING • GENERAL CONTROLLING • ACCOUNT ASSIGNMENT LOGIC • OKC9—DEFINE SUBSTITUTION

Two steps were created, one for the debit postings, and another for credit postings.

Step 1:

Prerequisite: RCL_ICCF-RACCT = '640000' AND RCL_ICCF-BEKNZ = 'C'

Substitute GL 450000

Step 2:

Prerequisite: RCL_ICCF-RACCT = '640000' AND RCL_ICCF-BEKNZ = 'D'

Substitute GL 450000

FI impact:

Resulting FI document will be posted as follows: (by way of CO-FI Reconciliation and use of CO Substitution)

▶ CO side:

Debit GL 640000, cost center C51101

Credit GL 640000, cost center C51900

▶ FI side:

Debit GL 450000, cost center C51101

Credit GL 450000, cost center C51900

"This is great. This is what we were looking for!" Frank said.

"Since we are selective in which cost element needs to be replaced, I believe we can do this," Alex replied. "If you had asked me to replace each and every secondary cost element with a corresponding GL Account, then it would not have been easy to achieve using this approach. I was checking with Erin and she informed me that SAP has addressed this requirement in the new Simple Finance functionality. Each secondary cost element is also created as a GL Account, that way we do not need to use such a substitution rule. But until we migrate to Simple Finance, we will have to use this option."

"I understand. Thanks for the explanation, Alex. This should work for my immediate requirement for reporting benefits accrual," Frank said.

6 Conclusion

"So we have had a successful year of integrating NCL into GCI's SAP system!" Bob congratulated the team during the celebration event. "We had some issues the month we went live, but thanks to the great efforts put in by the team, we now have a very stable platform," Bob said.

"What I particularly liked was the sharing of best practices between GCI and NCL teams. Alex and Frank, you both did a great job on this front. I know you have been in constant touch throughout the year! I appreciate your efforts. Erin, you too deserve a big share of the success. Thanks to your help, Alex learned all of our processes and systems very well during his first year at GCI. Additionally in his second year, Alex went on to coach Frank very effectively," Bob continued.

"I am so glad that our department is so efficient and is able to get the most out of the SAP system. I have seen the team improve on all of our metrics, including master data maintenance, transaction processing, month-end close, and reporting—we are completing our tasks quickly and efficiently. Speed and accuracy in our management reporting has helped our senior leadership make timely decisions, which in turn has helped contribute to the profitability of our organization. Kudos to everyone on the teamwork!" Bob made his concluding remarks.

Once the event was over, Erin, Alex, and Frank shared notes about the event and on what they felt would be the future of SAP design at GCI and NCL.

6.1   Direction of SAP Business Software

"Well, you must have heard about HANA, SAP's in-memory database. This is a great new technological innovation that is going to change the way we look at our transactions and reporting," Erin said.

"Really?" What does it do? How different is it from our current set up?" Frank was curious to know more about HANA.

"*SAP HANA* stores data in-memory. Which means that data resides in such a way that it can be read and retrieved quickly. Second, data is stored in a columnar format, rather than row format, which makes reading data even faster. A lot of performance issues that we see today should not be a concern with the new system," Erin replied.

"Oh wow! Does this mean that the performance optimization for our allocation cycles, material ledger close, and costing runs is of no use anymore?" Alex asked.

"Not really. Those improvements will not be undone, but the data retrieval and processing will be so fast that we will not even realize how quickly we complete our month-end close activities," Erin replied. "Like how SAP used to have R/2 until the 1990's; and then R/3 was introduced and later ECC. The new platform is called SAP *S/4HANA*."

6.2 Simple Finance, S/4HANA Finance

"This is very interesting," Alex replied. "Erin, are there any new features in Finance and Controlling that we should be aware of?"

"Yes, the redesigned Finance module is called *Simple Finance*, also known as *S/4HANA Finance* that will use the HANA technology features to expedite data retrieval and storage," Erin responded.

"This is great, does it perform allocations quickly? How about WIP, Variance, and Settlement transactions?" Frank wanted to know.

"Yes, they are all improved to a great extent. As you will remember, we have had to run a lot of jobs in background and sometimes even at an off-peak times to ensure it does not impact our system performance. With S/4HANA Finance, we can continue to use background processing, but it is not a must. Running in the foreground will provide an equally quick result!" Erin replied.

"Oh, so does this mean we will need to relook at our close schedule, and possibly other day-to-day tasks too?" Alex asked.

"Exactly. Processes as well as system tasks will need to be redesigned to some extent in order to use the new features effectively," Erin replied.

"This sounds very exciting!" Frank exclaimed. "I wonder if GCI and NCL will get to see this product soon."

"We are evaluating the roadmap to S/4HANA, we will see some definitive plans in the next few quarters. I myself do not have all that much insight into this product, but I have gathered some information by reading books and articles on this topic, by attending webinars, and in various discussions with our consulting partners," Erin responded. "It will be nice to see us move to the new tool. I can't wait!" Alex said.

6.3 Major changes in SAP Finance and Controlling

"Are there any major design improvements from a functionality standpoint? Alex asked.

"There are several. You may like to note that the *secondary cost element* is now going to be available in GL Account master," Erin said.

"Really? Then what happens to the secondary cost postings within CO?" Alex was curious.

"This is one big change that was made to ensure that all data in CO is also reflected in FI. Technically, the cost element category has been brought into GL Account master data. This will allow us to differentiate if this is a primary or secondary posting," Erin explained.

"Oh, I see. So the CO data is available in CO just like before. Is that correct?" Alex asked.

"Yes, that is right. CO does not go away, but feeds back to FI in real time, much like CO-FI real-time integration, but this time the master data is built into FI, which was not the case earlier. There was just one GL account representing the secondary postings, now we have many," Erin clarified.

"Another change you may like to know is around *index tables*. All index tables are removed and replaced with a view of the same name. Now there are just few primary tables which will store data. Since data is read in-memory, we do not have the performance constraint like before. Index tables were used to store replicated data in a summarized format, they are not necessary anymore. The views of the summarized table are available so that the existing reports built on these summarized tables will work in future," Erin explained another feature.

"Also, *account based CO-PA* is now a part of the S/4HANA Finance tables. One can continue to use *costing based CO-PA* if necessary, but it is not a must," Erin continued.

"There seems to be a trend here—a lot of design and functionality seems to be moving from CO to FI," Alex said. "As an example, when the new General Ledger was introduced, profit center functionality moved from CO to FI. Next, with Simple Finance, the attribute information for secondary cost element is going to be available in FI. Lastly, CO-PA information will now be a part of FI. All this makes me think that CO is losing importance," Alex continued.

"Well, your observations are partly correct, but as you will realize, when the functionality shifts from one module to another, it does not mean that the business requirement goes away. These changes are done to ensure that there is better data capture and reporting, at an efficient pace. These improvements are introduced based on the feedback received from so many customers like ours," Erin clarified.

"Let us look at all the projects we have worked on over the last few months. Each of the 35 projects we took was our answer to address a specific pain point that we had in configuration, master data, transaction data, month-end close, or reporting. Our business requirement remained the same, but the manner in which we addressed the requirement helped us work in an efficient manner," Erin continued.

"Similarly, when account-based CO-PA moves to FI, it may not eliminate the need of costing-based CO-PA. When a secondary cost element moves to FI, it will not eliminate the need for activity type and absorption on cost centers. The material ledger close procedure will still need to be performed in order get the *periodic unit price*. So whether the functionality shifts from FI to CO or from CO to FI does not eliminate the need for the business requirement as such. The expertise that we have gained over the last several years can be built further with these new tools and technology," Erin explained.

"Very lively discussion. I look forward to working with the new technology, learning more about the new features, and building further on my SAP knowledge," Alex concluded.

"Me too!" Frank exclaimed.

You have finished the book.

A   The Author

Ashish Sampat is a qualified finance and costing professional with more than two decades of industry experience in the SAP Finance and Controlling space. Ashish has been an SAP consultant for most of his career with various consulting organizations and now works as an independent SAP FI/CO consultant. He has provided solutions in several areas of SAP Controlling including product costing, material ledger, and cost center accounting to global clients in consumer packed goods, life sciences, and industrial sectors. Born and educated in India, Ashish now lives in suburban Chicago with his wife and two kids.

This is the second published book written by Ashish. The first was "First Steps in SAP Controlling (CO)," published by Espresso Tutorials.

B Index

C Disclaimer

This publication contains references to the products of SAP SE.

SAP, R/3, SAP NetWeaver, Duet, PartnerEdge, ByDesign, SAP BusinessObjects Explorer, StreamWork, and other SAP products and services mentioned herein as well as their respective logos are trademarks or registered trademarks of SAP SE in Germany and other countries.

Business Objects and the Business Objects logo, BusinessObjects, Crystal Reports, Crystal Decisions, Web Intelligence, Xcelsius, and other Business Objects products and services mentioned herein as well as their respective logos are trademarks or registered trademarks of Business Objects Software Ltd. Business Objects is an SAP company.

Sybase and Adaptive Server, iAnywhere, Sybase 365, SQL Anywhere, and other Sybase products and services mentioned herein as well as their respective logos are trademarks or registered trademarks of Sybase, Inc. Sybase is an SAP company.

SAP SE is neither the author nor the publisher of this publication and is not responsible for its content. SAP Group shall not be liable for errors or omissions with respect to the materials. The only warranties for SAP Group products and services are those that are set forth in the express warranty statements accompanying such products and services, if any. Nothing herein should be construed as constituting an additional warranty.

More Espresso Tutorials Books

Martin Munzel:

New SAP® Controlling Planning Interface

▶ Introduction to Netweaver Business Client

▶ Flexible Planning Layouts

▶ Plan Data Upload from Excel

http://5011.espresso-tutorials.com

Michael Esser:

Investment Project Controlling with SAP®

▶ SAP ERP functionality for investment controlling

▶ Concepts, roles and different scenarios

▶ Effective planning and reporting

http://5008.espresso-tutorials.com

Stefan Eifler:

Quick Guide to SAP® CO-PA (Profitability Analysis)

▶ Basic organizational entities and master data

▶ Define the actual value flow

▶ Set up a planning environment

▶ Create your own reports

http://5018.espresso-tutorials.com

Kermit Bravo & Scott Cairncross:

SAP® Enterprise Performance Management (EPM) Add-In

- ▶ Learn about the Connection Concept
- ▶ Get familiar with the SAP EPM Add-In for Excel and BPC 10.1
- ▶ Create a Basic Report from Scratch
- ▶ Walk through a Detailed Case Study

http://5042.espresso-tutorials.com

Paul Ovigele:

Reconciling SAP® CO-PA to the General Ledger

- ▶ Learn the Difference between Costing-based and Accounting-based CO-PA
- ▶ Walk through Various Value Flows into CO-PA
- ▶ Match the Cost-of-Sales Account with Corresponding Value Fields in CO-PA

http://5040.espresso-tutorials.com

Tanya Duncan:

Practical Guide to SAP® CO-PC (Product Cost Controlling)

- ▶ Cost Center Planning Process and Costing Run Execution
- ▶ Actual Cost Analysis & Reporting
- ▶ Controlling Master Data
- ▶ Month End Processes in Details

http://5064.espresso-tutorials.com

Ashish Sampat:

First Steps in SAP® Controlling (CO)

- ▶ Cost center and product cost planning and actual cost flow
- ▶ Best practices for cost absorption using Product Cost Controlling
- ▶ Month-end closing activities in SAP Controlling
- ▶ Examples and screenshots based on a case study approach

http://5069.espresso-tutorials.com

Rosana Fonseca:

Practical Guide to SAP® Material Ledger (ML)

- ▶ SAP Material Ledger functionality and key integration points
- ▶ Tips for implementing and using SAP ML effectively
- ▶ The most important SAP Material Ledger reports, including CKM3N
- ▶ Detailed steps for executing a multilevel actual costing run

http://5116.espresso-tutorials.com

Tanya Duncan:

The Essential SAP® Career Guide—Hitting the Ground Running

- ▶ Fundamentals of an SAP job search
- ▶ Interviews with leading SAP professionals in diverse career paths
- ▶ Tips for choosing the right SAP module for you
- ▶ Important SAP skills & tools

http://5142.espresso-tutorials.com